ABIDE IN CHRIST

IN TODAY'S ENGLISH WITH INTRODUCTION AND STUDY GUIDE

ANDREW MURRAY

GODLIPRESS TEAM

© COPYRIGHT 2021 BY GODLIPRESS.

All rights reserved. The content contained within this book may not be reproduced, duplicated, or transmitted without direct written permission from the author or the publisher, except in the case of brief quotations embodied in critical articles or reviews.

Scripture quotations are from The ESV® Bible (The Holy Bible, English Standard Version®), copyright © 2001 by Crossway, a publishing ministry of Good News Publishers. Used by permission. All rights reserved.

GodliPress exists to glorify God and to encourage believers in their walk with Christ. We do not necessarily endorse all doctrinal views of the authors we publish. Our hope and earnest prayer is that you find our updated editions of the Christian classics much easier to understand and that God would bless you through any teaching in them that is in line with the Gospel as revealed in His Word.

CONTENTS

Introduction — vii
Preface — xi

1. YOU WHO HAVE COME TO CHRIST — 1
   Study Guide — 5

2. FIND REST FOR YOUR SOUL — 7
   Study Guide — 12

3. TRUSTING CHRIST TO KEEP YOU — 14
   Study Guide — 18

4. THE BRANCH IN THE VINE — 20
   Study Guide — 24

5. YOU CAME TO CHRIST BY FAITH — 26
   Study Guide — 32

6. GOD HAS UNITED YOU TO CHRIST — 34
   Study Guide — 38

7. CHRIST AS YOUR WISDOM — 40
   Study Guide — 45

8. CHRIST AS YOUR RIGHTEOUSNESS — 47
   Study Guide — 52

9. CHRIST AS YOUR SANCTIFICATION — 54
   Study Guide — 60

10. CHRIST AS YOUR REDEMPTION — 62
    Study Guide — 66

11. CHRIST THE CRUCIFIED ONE — 68
    Study Guide — 73

12. GOD WILL ESTABLISH YOU IN CHRIST   74
   Study Guide   79

13. EVERY MOMENT   81
   Study Guide   85

14. DAY BY DAY   87
   Study Guide   91

15. AT THIS MOMENT   93
   Study Guide   98

16. FORSAKING ALL FOR CHRIST   99
   Study Guide   104

17. THROUGH THE HOLY SPIRIT   105
   Study Guide   110

18. IN STILLNESS OF SOUL   111
   Study Guide   115

19. IN SUFFERING AND HARDSHIP   117
   Study Guide   121

20. THAT YOU MAY BEAR MUCH FRUIT   123
   Study Guide   128

21. SO YOU WILL HAVE POWER IN PRAYER   129
   Study Guide   133

22. AND IN CHRIST'S LOVE   135
   Study Guide   139

23. AS CHRIST IN THE FATHER   141
   Study Guide   145

24. OBEYING HIS COMMANDMENTS   147
   Study Guide   152

25. THAT YOUR JOY MAY BE FULL   153
   Study Guide   157

26. AND IN LOVE TO ONE ANOTHER   159
   Study Guide   163

27. THAT YOU MAY NOT SIN	165
Study Guide	171
28. CHRIST AS YOUR STRENGTH	172
Study Guide	177
29. AND NOT IN SELF	179
Study Guide	185
30. CHRIST AS GUARANTEE OF THE COVENANT	187
Study Guide	191
31. CHRIST THE GLORIFIED ONE	193
Study Guide	197
About Andrew Murray	199
References	201

INTRODUCTION

Abide in Christ is not just another teaching or a devotional, but consists of rich revelation that is so significant for Christians today. Originally, with the subtitle: *Thoughts on the Blessed Life of Fellowship With the Son of God,* it is clear that with this book, Andrew Murray sought to open hearts and minds to the possibility that there is more for us in our lives with Christ than we realize.

In the book of John, there are only a few chapters between the Last Supper and Jesus being arrested, and yet these are some of the most vital words recorded in the Bible. The Teacher finally explains everything to His disciples, knowing He will leave them soon. His last words are a series of instructions, analogies, warnings, and encouragements. Jesus took the time to lay out a clear blueprint for the Christian life as God intended in its fullness.

Living life to the fullest in God is something we all aspire to, or generally just wish we had. A close, continuous relationship with Him is the culmination of our spiritual journey. But thinking and knowing about it, and actually doing and living it is often where most of us stall and lose our way. In the end, we opt to lead mediocre Christian lives, hoping it's enough. But if we look closely, Jesus uses a simple analogy, with incredible ramifications and blessings if we can understand and follow it.

The parable of the vine and the branches is not new to us and is even used in non-Christian circles to illustrate the benefits of tapping in, being grafted, and drawing strength from a relationship bigger than ourselves. But as with anything Jesus said, the simplicity of it hides the incredible treasures of what He really meant for us as disciples, followers, branches.

Often, we get confused about what our part is: As a branch, how hard must I try, what must I do, how long must I carry on before I see fruit? And what is Jesus' part: As the Vine, what does He do, what has He already done, how does He do it in my heart, can I trust Him to do it?

To read any Andrew Murray book is to know that you will not only learn but be deeply challenged. Often, with his books, it requires reading the same chapter over and again, just to let the full revelation of what he is saying, sink in. Not one to mince his words, Murray combined practical applications with Scripture to reveal what all of us should know, and need to know about living the Christian life. This guide is no different.

Written over a century ago, it has stood up against a landslide of Christian expository and self-help books that fill our bookstores. It continues to be read and treasured by pastors, teachers, and Christians who desire to experience fruitful lives in Jesus. As a classic, the heart and message of *Abide in Christ* remain, while the language has been modified only to make it more accessible to present-day readers.

Murray's presentation of the concept in a 31-day devotional is typical of his practical approach to helping day-to-day Christians like us. In bite-sized chunks, this simple, yet complex idea of the branches and the vine is broken down into portions we can digest as daily food. By sticking to this outline, the benefits of meditating and absorbing what he has to say, coupled with verses, will definitely bring the reader to a deeper understanding of what it means to live in Christ. The best way to read this is as a daily guide, one chapter a day, committed from start to finish.

The study guide has been added into this publication of the book for extra insight and reflection, either for yourself or as a group. It is not meant to add or distract from the text, but rather to direct our attention to looking back at what we have just read and think a little deeper on it, and see how it applies to our own lives. In doing so, we will move closer to an understanding and, hopefully, a living of Jesus' words. As we do so, we will begin to bear much fruit and bring Him glory, just as He intended.

PREFACE

The words Jesus used most when talking about His disciples' relationship to Himself, were "Follow me." He used new words when He was about to go back to heaven. A more intimate and spiritual union between them and His glory is expressed in these words: "Abide in me."

Unfortunately, the meaning of these words, and the blessed life it promises, are hidden from many sincere followers of Jesus. They trust in Him as their Saviour for forgiveness and help, as well as trying to obey Him. But they don't quite realize the close fellowship and wonderful life that He invited them into when He said, "Abide in me." It's not only an incredible loss for them, but for the church and the world too.

We might ask why those who have accepted Jesus as Saviour and have access to the Holy Spirit's renewing power don't take hold of the full salvation that has been prepared for them. Ignorance is normally the answer. If abiding in Christ —living in and with Him to experience His continuous presence and care—were preached with the same clarity and urgency as salvation and forgiveness, many would accept this invitation. We would see it manifest itself in their lives through purity and power, love and joy, fruitfulness, and every blessing connected to abiding in Him.

This book is to help those who haven't fully understood what Jesus meant with this command, or they think it's beyond their reach. Just like children that only learn lessons if they are repeated again and again, if you constantly fix your minds on some of these lessons of faith, you will eventually understand and live them. I hope that some—especially new Christians—will find it helpful reading a chapter a day over the next month and meditating on the words, "Abide in me," and the lessons from the parable of the vine.

Step by step, we shall see how this promise is meant for us: There is grace to help us obey it; experiencing its blessing is vital to living a healthy Christian life; incredible blessings flow from it. As we listen, meditate, and pray—surrender ourselves and accept in faith all of Jesus—the Holy Spirit will make the words real to us. These words of Jesus will become the power of God unto salvation for us, and through them, we will have faith to take hold of the full blessing.

I pray that our gracious Lord will bless this book and help those who seek to know Him fully (as He has in previous editions). I also pray that He would make all those Christians who are not living full lives see how He is drawing them to Himself and that if they surrender themselves completely to abide in Him, what incredible joy and glory they will experience. Those of us who have tasted some of the sweetness of this life, be witnesses of the grace and power Jesus has to keep us united with Himself. Let us win others in our actions and words to follow Him fully. We must bear this fruit to keep abiding in Him—they can't be separate.

One word of advice to my reader: It takes time to grow into Jesus the Vine. Don't expect to do so unless you give Him that time. It's not enough to read the Bible or this book. Then, when we think we understand everything and have asked God for His blessing, to go out hoping it will work. It needs to be day by day with Jesus.

It's the same with our meal times each day—we need at least an hour for dinner, not to eat our food in a hurry. *"If we are to live through Jesus, we must feed on Him,"* (John 6:57). We must take in everything and digest the heavenly food the Father has given us in His life. So, if we want to learn to abide in Jesus, we must take time each day, before, while, and after reading, to put ourselves in living contact with the living Jesus. We must consciously surrender to His influence. If we give Him the opportunity to take hold of us, He will draw us up and keep us safe in His almighty life.

To all the Christians He gives me the privilege to point toward the Heavenly Vine, I give you brotherly love and greetings, praying that each of you may be given the rich and full experience of abiding in Christ. May the grace of Jesus, the love of God, and the fellowship of the Holy Spirit be your daily portion. Amen.

Andrew Murray

John 15:1-12

"I am the true vine, and my Father is the vinedresser.

Every branch in me that does not bear fruit he takes away, and every branch that does bear fruit he prunes, that it may bear more fruit. Already you are clean because of the word that I have spoken to you. Abide in me, and I in you. As the branch cannot bear fruit by itself, unless it abides in the vine, neither can you, unless you abide in me. I am the vine; you are the branches.

Whoever abides in me and I in him, he it is that bears much fruit, for apart from me you can do nothing. If anyone does not abide in me he is thrown away like a branch and withers; and the branches are gathered, thrown into the fire, and burned. If you abide in me, and my words abide in you, ask whatever you wish, and it will be done for you. By this my Father is glorified, that you bear much fruit and so prove to be my disciples. As the Father has loved me, so have I loved you. Abide in my love.

If you keep my commandments, you will abide in my love, just as I have kept my Father's commandments and abide in his love. These things I have spoken to you, that my joy may be in you, and that your joy may be full. This is my commandment, that you love one another as I have loved you."

1

YOU WHO HAVE COME TO CHRIST

"Come to me." –Matthew 11:28
"Abide in me." –John 15:4

For those who have heard and responded to the call, "Come to me," a new invitation comes, "Abide in me." They are both from the same loving Saviour. If you have responded, you have probably not regretted doing so. His word is truth, His promises He fulfills, and His blessings and love are yours to experience. His welcome is warm, His pardon full and free, His love sweet and precious. More than once, since accepting the invitation, you have said, "No one told me it would be this amazing."

And yet, as time went on, you have been disappointed because your expectations were not met. The blessings you once enjoyed are lost. The love and joy when you first met Jesus have become shallow and weak, not deep as you hoped.

You have often wondered why. With such a mighty and loving Saviour, shouldn't your experience of salvation be much fuller?

The answer is simple: You wandered away from Him. The blessings He gives are all connected with His "Come to <u>me</u>." They can only be enjoyed in close fellowship with Him. Maybe you didn't fully understand, or forgot that the call meant, "Come to me to stay with me." This was what He meant when He first called you. It was not to refresh you with His love and deliverance for a few hours after you were born again, only to let you carry on into sadness and sin. He destined you to something better than brief moments of joy and blessings that can only be found in special times of prayer, that disappear as you carry on with your day-to-day lives.

No. He prepared a place for you to abide with Him, where every moment of your entire life may be spent. The work of your daily life is meant to happen here, where you enjoy a constant relationship with Him. Just as Jesus said, "Come to me," He made everything clear by adding, "Abide in me." As sincere and faithful, loving and tender, as the compassion that breathed "Come," was the grace that added, "Abide." The call that first attracted and drew you in was mighty, just like the second invitation that is powerful enough to keep you. The blessings you received when you came to Jesus were great, but the treasures that abiding in Him unlocks are much greater.

He didn't say, "Abide <u>with</u> me," but "Abide <u>in</u> me." It is meant to be an intimate and complete relationship. He opened His arms to take you in. He opened His heart to welcome you there. All His divine life and love were offered to make you one with Himself. We have not fully realized the depth of what He means by these words: "Abide <u>in me</u>."

If you had noticed, the heart which He says, "Come to me" is the same in "Abide in me." Your motivations to respond to the first should be the same to answer the second.

What drew you to Jesus, fear of sin and its curse? The forgiveness you received when you first came to Him, with all the blessings, could only be confirmed and enjoyed by abiding in Him. Did you have a longing to know and enjoy His love that called to you that first time? That was just a taste—the real satisfaction of a thirsty soul that drinks of His blessings are only found in abiding. Were you tired of the bondage of sin, longing to be free, pure, and holy, and find God's rest for your soul? The rest Jesus gives can only be realized if you abide in Him.

Maybe you responded because of the hope of an inheritance and being in His presence in heaven. Preparing for that day, and its enjoyments in this life, are only given to those who abide in Him. There is nothing that motivates you to respond, that does not compel you, even more, to "Abide in Him." You did well to come; you do better to abide. Who would be happy just to stand in the door of the King's Palace when he is invited to go in and live in the King's presence, sharing all the glory of His royal life? Let us enter in and abide, and enjoy everything His wonderful love has prepared for us!

Unfortunately, many have come to Jesus, only to confess that they hardly know anything of truly abiding in Him. For some, the reason is that they never fully understood what Jesus meant by these words. For others who heard, they didn't know that such a life of abiding fellowship was possible, and within reach. Others will say that even though they believed such a life was possible and looked for it, they haven't found the secret to get there. Still, others will blame their own unfaithfulness for keeping them from enjoying this blessing. They were not prepared to give up everything to abide in Him completely, even though Jesus longs to abide with them.

To each of these different people, I come in the name of Jesus with the message: "Abide in me." In His name, I invite all of us to meditate on the meaning, lessons, claims, and promises that go with this invitation. I know there are many questions that will come up when we look at it, especially for new Christians. The obvious question is how to keep in or keep up this abiding relationship during work, daily tasks, and distractions.

I cannot remove all the difficulties that arise as we look at these words. Jesus alone must do this by His Holy Spirit. If we repeat His command every day, God's power and grace will settle the words "Abide in me" into our hearts until it finds a place where it will not be forgotten or neglected anymore. We should meditate on its meaning as we read the Bible until the understanding that unlocks the heart reveals what it offers and expects. We will discover how to abide in Christ, what keeps us from doing so, and what can help us to do it.

Jesus' claim on our lives should be strong enough to bring us to see that allegiance to the King means accepting all His commands—this one too. As we seek it and its blessings, our hearts will be stirred to take hold of this invitation and all it offers to us.

Let us sit at His feet, and meditate on this word, looking on nothing else but Him. Let us be quiet, waiting to hear the still small voice that is mightier than the storm and breaks the rocks. The heart that hears Jesus saying "Abide in me" receives power to accept and hold the blessing He offers.

Speak to us, blessed Savior, let each of us hear Your voice. May our deep need and the faith of Your love, combined with the vision of the blessed life You want to give us, bring us to listen and to obey, as often as we hear You say "Abide in me." Every day, let our hearts answer clearer and clearer: "Blessed Savior, I do abide in You. "

STUDY GUIDE

These questions are meant to guide discussion and reflection on what you have just read, and not as an examination to work through and pass! So, approach them with an open mind, add your own thoughts, and if they lead you on to further questions and more discussion, then they have achieved their purpose. Answer on your own, or in a Bible study group. Work through them at your own pace.

1. Do you see any similarity in Jesus calling His disciples to calling us to follow Him? (see Matt 4:19)
2. Looking at your own salvation, when you were born

again and came to Christ, you may not have distinctly heard the words "Come to me," but do you remember that He called you to Him? Describe how this happened.
3. Murray talks about a disappointment that we sometimes experience after coming to Him. He says the answer to why this happens is simple. Do you agree with him?
4. What is the difference between the two commands: "Come to me" and "Abide in me?"
5. Murray talks about much greater blessings that come when we move from responding to the first call, and on to the second. What blessings would these be?
6. He mentions questions that will arise once we begin to look at abiding in Him. What questions do you have at the start of this book?

2

FIND REST FOR YOUR SOUL

"Come to me, all who labor and are heavy laden, and I will give you rest. Take my yoke upon you, and learn from me, for I am gentle and lowly in heart, and you will find rest for your souls."
–Matthew 11:28-29

Rest for the soul. This was the promise Jesus offered to burdened sinners. It sounds simple, but it is much greater and more complex. It means being delivered from fear, having our needs and desires met. Jesus offers all this to anyone who is lost and disappointed that they have not found His rest—as a prize to come back and abide in Him. There is only one reason that the rest was not found, or lost since finding it: You did not abide with and in Him.

In the first invitation to come to Jesus, the promise of rest was repeated twice. But the difference in conditions suggests that abiding rest could only be found in an abiding relationship. First He says, "Come to me, and I will give you rest." The moment you come and believe, He will give you rest—forgiveness and acceptance in His love. But everything that God gives us needs time to become completely ours. We have to hold on to it and absorb it into our hearts. There is no other way that His gifts to us will become ours to experience and enjoy to the fullest.

So, Jesus repeats His promise, but instead of speaking of the rest for the weary one who comes, He talks of a deeper, personal rest of the soul that abides with Him. he goes further than just saying "Come to me" and adds "Take my yoke upon you and learn from me." In other words, become my students, be trained by me, submit everything to my will, and let your whole life be one with me—abide in me. He doesn't just say "I will give," but also "you shall find rest for your souls." The rest He gave when you first came to Him will become personal—a deeper abiding rest that comes from a close relationship and complete surrender. "Take my yoke, and learn from me," "Abide in me"—this is the path to abiding rest.

Don't Jesus' words reveal what you always ask—how this rest that you have felt is often lost? Perhaps because you didn't understand that complete surrender to Him is the secret to perfect rest. It means giving up your whole life to Him, to rule and have His way. It means taking up His yoke and submitting to be led and taught by Him. It means abiding in Him, to be and do only what He wills. These conditions of discipleship are the only way to maintain the rest that was given when you first came to Christ. The rest is in Christ, and not something He gives apart from Himself. It is only in having Jesus that the rest can really be kept and enjoyed.

As new Christians, many of us don't grasp this truth, so the rest disappears so quickly. For some, we never really knew because we were never taught that Jesus demands the undivided allegiance of the whole heart and life. We didn't understand that He wants to reign over every single part of our lives; that even in the smallest things, we must seek to please Him. We didn't know how completely Jesus wants us to be set apart for Him.

For others, we had some idea of the holy life Christians should live. But the mistake was we didn't believe it was possible to achieve. Taking up the yoke, bearing it, and never laying it down was beyond our efforts and our reach. Always, all the day, abiding in Jesus, was only something we might be able to do after a lifetime of holiness and growth, not a weak beginner.

We didn't know that Jesus was telling the truth when He said, "My yoke is easy." The yoke gives the rest because as soon as the heart submits in obedience, the Lord gives the strength and joy to do it. We didn't notice that He added, "I am meek and lowly in heart" when He said, "Learn of me." He wanted to reassure us that His gentleness would meet all our needs and care for us as a mother does for her child. We didn't know that His love would hold, keep, and bless us if we surrendered when He said, "Abide in me."

Just as some have failed to completely set themselves apart in holiness, others have failed because they didn't fully trust. These two, consecration and faith, are the essential elements of the Christian life—giving up all to Jesus, receiving all from Jesus. They are expressed in each other and united in one word: Surrender. Full surrender is to obey as well as to trust, to trust as well as to obey.

It's no surprise that our lives are not filled with joy or strength as we had hoped. At times, we've been led into sin without knowing it because we hadn't learned how Jesus wanted to reign completely in us, and how we couldn't stay on the path unless He was very near. At other times, we knew what sin was, but had no power to conquer it because we didn't know or believe how Jesus would completely come in to keep and help us.

It wasn't long before the joy of our first love was lost, and instead of our path shining more and more to that perfect day, it became like Israel's wandering in the desert—walking, not too far, and yet always just short of the promised rest. Weary souls roaming about like the thirsty deer, come and learn that there is a place where safety and victory, peace and rest, are always certain. That place is always open to you— the heart of Jesus.

There is an argument that abiding in Jesus, bearing His yoke, learning of Him, is so difficult, and the effort to achieve it is more disruptive to the rest than sin or the world. It is not true and, yet, many share this view! Is it tiring for a traveler to rest on a bed when he is tired? Or is it an effort for a little child to rest in its mother's arms? Is it not the house that keeps the traveler within its shelter? Don't the arms of the mother sustain and keep the little one? So it is with Jesus. The soul just has to submit to Him, be still, and rest knowing that His love and faithfulness will keep it safe. The blessing is so great that often our little hearts can't take hold of it. It's as if we can't believe that Jesus, the Almighty One, will actually teach and keep us all day. But this is exactly what He has promised, for without this He can't give us rest.

When He says "Abide in me," "Learn of me," He really means it. And when our hearts take this in and believe that it's His job to keep us abiding when we surrender to Him, then we throw ourselves into His loving arms. It's not the yoke, but resistance to the yoke, that brings the difficulty. The wholehearted surrender to Jesus, our Master and Keeper, will find and secure the rest.

Come, let us accept the simple words of Jesus. The command is specific: "Take my yoke, and learn of me," "Abide in me. " A command has to be obeyed. The obedient student asks no questions about possibilities or results but accepts every order, confident that the teacher has provided everything that is needed. The power and the perseverance to abide in the rest, and the blessing in abiding, is the Saviour's responsibility. We must obey, He must provide.

Let us obediently accept the command and boldly answer, "Jesus, I abide in You. I will take Your yoke immediately. I abide in You." Instead of thinking of failure, let us focus on the urgency of the command, to listen until the Spirit opens our ears to hear Jesus saying, with a love and authority that inspires hope and obedience, "Child, abide in me." Those words will end our doubts—a promise of what will be given. In its simplicity, we will understand it clearly. Abiding in

Jesus is giving up of ourselves to be ruled, taught, and led—to rest in the arms of Everlasting Love.

The fruit and the fellowship of God's own rest are only found in those who come to Jesus to abide in Him. It's the peace of God, the great calm of the eternal world, that passes all understanding, and keeps the heart and mind. With this grace, we have strength for every duty, courage for every struggle, a blessing in every cross, and the joy of life eternal in death itself.

Oh my Savior, if my heart should doubt or fear again because the expectation was too great or achieving it was too far, let me hear Your voice to build up my faith and obedience: "Abide in me"; "*Take my yoke upon you, and learn from me; you will find rest for your souls.*"

STUDY GUIDE

A good idea is to keep a notebook close by as you work through these daily devotions. Not only to keep a record of your thoughts and answers but also to revisit and be surprised and reminded of the growth or wisdom you have gained since you wrote them down. Being as honest as you can with your notes will really help this type of exercise.

1. Rest for our physical bodies and rest for our souls are very different. In your opinion, what is the difference between the two?
2. The verse, Matt 11:28-29, talks about two kinds of rest for the soul. What are they?
3. What is meant by a yoke? It will be good to research

its meaning to give you some context of this picture. Why does Jesus use this image?
4. Murray says that it's not the yoke that brings difficulty. What does he pinpoint as the problem?
5. What do you understand by the statement: "Giving up all to Jesus, receiving all from Jesus?"
6. According to Murray, what is full surrender?

3

TRUSTING CHRIST TO KEEP YOU

"I press on to make it my own, because Christ Jesus has made me his own."
–Philippians 3:12

Many of us agree it's a duty and privilege to abide in Christ. But we always hesitate when the question is asked: Is continuous fellowship with Jesus possible? Maybe for those prominent Christians who've been given time and grace to learn it, but for us with busy lives, it seems impossible. The more we hear about this life and its glory and blessings, the more we want it. But we are too weak and unfaithful. We'll never achieve it.

However, abiding in Christ is meant for weak Christians as well, especially because they are weak. It doesn't depend on doing great things and doesn't require us to first be holy and devoted. No, it's simply a weak person trusting the Mighty

One to be kept—the unfaithful one fully surrendering to the One who is trustworthy and true. Abiding in Him is not work that we have to do in order to enjoy His salvation, but allowing Him to do everything for us, and in us, and through us. It's a work He does for us—the fruit and power of His redeeming love. Our part is simply to yield, trust, and wait for what He has planned to do.

A quiet expectation and confidence, resting on His promise of having prepared a place for us to abide—this is what many Christians don't have. They hardly have time to realize that when He says "Abide in me," He offers Himself. He is the One that never sleeps, with all His power and love, as the place the heart can live, where His grace is stronger to keep them than their tendency to stray. Their idea of grace is that their conversion and pardon are God's work, but it's now their job to live as Christians and follow Jesus. They must now do something, and even though they pray for help, it's still theirs to do. They fail continually and become hopeless. This only increases the helplessness.

No, it was Jesus who drew you when He said "Come," so it is Jesus who keeps you when He says "Abide." The grace to come and the grace to abide both come from Him. Hearing the call to come and accepting it, was love that drew you close. The call to abide is the band that keeps and holds you to Himself. Take time to listen to Jesus. "In me," He says, "is your place—in my almighty arms. I am the One that loves you and calls you to abide in me. Surely, you can trust me." Hearing this, we can only respond by saying, "Yes, Savior, in You, I can, I will abide."

. . .

Abide in me: These words are not the law of Moses that demands something from sinners that they cannot do. These words are the command of love that is a different kind of promise. If you think about this long enough until there is no feeling of fear and despair, then as you hear Him call you to abide, the first thought will be of hope: It's for me, I know I shall enjoy it. You are not under the law, with its persistent demand to 'do.' You are under grace, that says, "Believe that Jesus will do it for you." And if we ask, "But surely there is something for us to do?" The answer is, "Anything we do, is the fruit of His work in us." When our hearts rest on what Jesus will do, then we are inspired to work because we know He works in us. When we see the power and love of being "in Him," we are motivated to abide in Him.

Paul expresses this connection between Christ's work and our work in "*I press on to make it my own, because Christ Jesus has made me his own*," (Phil 3:2). He knew that God was mighty and faithful to make him one with Himself, and so he did everything he could to achieve the glorious prize. The faith, experience, and assurance that "*Jesus has made me his own*," gave him the courage and strength to press on and take hold of what he was called to. Each revelation of what Jesus had planned for him, motivated him to aim at nothing less.

We can understand Paul's expression and application in our lives when we think of a father helping his child climb a steep cliff. The father stands above and is holding his son's hand to help him. He points to the spot where he must put his feet so he can jump up. The leap is too high and dangerous, but the father's hand is his trust. The boy jumps to get to the point that his father has taken hold of him to get to. It's the father's strength that secures and lifts him up, and so urges him to use all his strength.

It's the same between Christ and us. First, we must fix our eyes on what He has called us to. It's a life of an abiding relationship with Himself that He wants to lift us to. Everything we already have—forgiveness, peace, the Spirit, and His grace—is in preparation for this. Everything else that has been promised—holiness, fruitfulness, and glory-are its conclusion. Jesus' main aim is to bring us into a relationship with Him and the Father. Fix your eye on this until it is very clear: Christ's aim is to have me abiding in Him.

Then we can think about what He has called me to. His power wants to lift me to where the place He wants me to be. Fix your eyes on Christ and His love that asks you to trust Him, the One that found and brought you close to keep you in Him. Gaze on that mighty hand that is able to keep you abiding in Him.

As you look to the place He is pointing to, keep your gaze fixed on Him holding you and waiting to lift you up. Is it not possible to take the step today, and enter into a life of abiding in Christ? Yes, start now. Say, "Jesus, if You ask me, and will lift and keep me there, I will go. Trembling, but trusting, I will say: Jesus, I abide in You."

I won't even speak about abiding in Him if all it does is stir up a religious response. God's truth must be acted on immediately. Surrender to the one thing He asks of you: Give yourself up to abide in Him. He will work it in you. You can trust Him to keep you trusting and abiding.

And if you doubt or past failures discourage you, just remember where Paul found His strength: *"Jesus has made me his own."* That is a fountain of strength that allows you to look up to the place Jesus has set His heart and your heart. From that you find the confidence that the good work He began, He will also complete. And in that confidence, you will find the courage to say, "I follow on, that I may also gain that for which Jesus has gained me." It's because Jesus has taken hold of you and keeps you, that you can say: "Savior, I abide in You."

STUDY GUIDE

Don't feel that you need to stick to the sequence of questions, or that you have to fulfill each one. Rather, let them be starting points that can open up and lead you to more thoughts on the passage, or more discussions around the topics. Some questions may take longer to digest and find answers. Take your time there before moving on, as it is better to allow the Holy Spirit to reveal things to you than simply ticking off the boxes.

1. "Is continuous fellowship with Jesus possible?" What is your answer to this?
2. God's work is to bring us to salvation, and now it's our job to live and follow Him. Is this your view of the Christian life?
3. What is God's work and what is our work?
4. Murray uses an image of a father helping a child to climb. Picture yourself in the place of the child

trusting God. What are your fears? What are your hopes?
5. The words, "Keep your gaze" and "Fix your eyes" are used here often. What exactly do these mean? How do you do this? (see Heb 12:2)
6. What do you think of having Paul as an example? It's often a daunting one to have as he sets the bar very high for the rest of us to follow. And, yet, he said to Christians weak and strong, *"Be imitators of me, as I am of Christ"* (1 Cor 11:1).

4

THE BRANCH IN THE VINE

"I am the vine; you are the branches." –John 15:5

Jesus first used the words "abide in me" when talking about the parable of the Vine. Such a simple, yet deep parable, that gives us the best and most complete picture of His command, and the relationship into which He invites us.

It teaches us that the connection between the vine and the branch is a living one. No external, temporary relationship will do. No work of man can bring it about. Whether the branch is an original or an engrafted one, it's only by Jesus' doing. The life, sap, and fruitfulness of the vine are what give the branch any life.

It's the same with Christians. Our relationship with Jesus has nothing to do with our wisdom or our strength, but it's all because of God. It's the only way a close and complete relationship between Jesus and a sinner can happen. "*God has sent the Spirit of his Son into our hearts*" (Gal 4:6). The same Spirit which lived and still lives in the Son becomes the life of the believer. In the unity of the Spirit, and fellowship of life in Christ, the sinner becomes one with Him. As between the vine and branch, it is a relationship that makes them one.

The parable teaches us the completeness of the relationship. So close is the union between the vine and the branch that they are nothing without each other, and live only for each other.

Without the vine, the branch can do nothing. Its place in the vineyard, its life, and its fruitfulness is owed to the vine. Jesus says, "*Apart from me you can do nothing*" (John 15:5). The Christian can only be pleasing to God when things are done through the power of Christ living in him. The only way to bear fruit is through the daily life of the Holy Spirit in him. Living only in Him and depending only on Him.

Without the branch, the vine can also do nothing. A vine without branches can't bear fruit. The vine is as important to the branches, as the branches to the vine. This is the wonderful grace of Jesus, that as we are dependent on Him, He has made Himself dependent on us. Without His disciples, His blessings can't be given to the world. This is the honor He gives us: As we rely on Him in heaven for our fruit, so He relies on us here on earth, to show fruit to everyone. Think on this until your heart bows before the mystery of the perfect union between Christ and the believer.

There is more: As the vine and branch are nothing without each other, so they also exist only for each other.

Everything the vine has belongs to the branches. The vine doesn't take nutrients and food from the soil for itself—everything is for the use of the branches. The parent is the servant of the branches. And Jesus, to whom we owe our life, completely gives Himself for us: "*The glory that you have given me I have given to them;*" "*Whoever believes in me will also do the works that I do; and greater works than these will he do*" (John 17:22, 14:12). His fullness and riches are for us. The vine doesn't live or keep things for itself but exists only for the branches. All that Jesus is in heaven, He is for us. He has no interest apart from ours. He stands before the Father as our representative.

All the branch has belongs to the vine. The branch doesn't exist for itself, but to bear fruit to show the excellence of the vine. It has no reason to exist, except to serve the vine. As Jesus gives Himself completely to us, we are motivated to be completely His. Our entire being, every moment of our lives, every thought, and feeling, belong to Jesus. From Him and for Him we might bear fruit. As we realize what the vine is to the branch, and what the branch is meant to be to the vine, we feel that we have one thing to think of and live for: The will, glory, work, and kingdom of Jesus-bearing fruit to glorify Him.

The parable teaches us the reason for the union. The branches are only there for fruit. "*Every branch in me that does not bear fruit he takes away*" (John 15:2). The branch needs leaves to sustain its life and to bear perfect fruit, which is to be given away to those around. When a Christian agrees to be a branch, he has to forget himself and live entirely for others. Jesus came to love, seek, and save them-every branch on the Vine has to live for his reason as much as the Vine itself. It's for fruit that the Father has made us one with Jesus.

Jesus, the living Vine in heaven, and I, the living branch on earth! How little we have understood of our great need and claim to His fullness! How little we have understood of His great need and claim to my emptiness!

Study this wonderful relationship between Jesus and His people, until it leads you into complete union with Him. Listen and believe, until everything in you says "Jesus is my True Vine, bearing, nourishing, supplying, using, and filling me to bear abundant fruit." Then you won't be afraid to say, "I am a branch to Jesus, the True Vine, abiding in Him, resting on Him, waiting for Him, serving Him that His grace and fruit be given to the world."

When we understand the parable in this way, His command that goes with it will become powerful to us. Understanding what the vine is to the branch, and Jesus to the believer will reveal the truth of the words, "Abide in me!" It will be as if He says, "Think how completely I belong to you. I have joined myself to you—all the fulness of the Vine are yours. Now that you are in me, all I have is yours. My desire and honor are to have you as a fruitful branch—only Abide in me. You are weak, but I am strong; you are poor, but I am rich-only abide in me. Surrender completely to my teaching and rule. Trust my love, grace, and promises. Only believe—I am yours. I am the Vine, you are the branch. Abide in me."

What can you say to that? Will you hesitate or think about it? Instead of thinking how hard and difficult it is to live like a branch of the True Vine because you thought it was something you had to accomplish, start seeing it as the most blessed and joyful thing under heaven. Now that you are in Him, He will keep and help you to abide. Your part is accepting and surrendering to the strong Vine to hold the weak branch.

Oh Savior, how incredible is Your love! "Such knowledge is too wonderful for me: It is high, I cannot attain it." I can only surrender myself to Your love every day, knowing that You reveal its precious mysteries to me, and so encourage and strengthen me to do what my heart desires—to abide completely in You.

STUDY GUIDE

It will be very helpful to have your Bible open and handy as you read through this chapter, and as you work through these questions. Rather than key verses, you can see them in their full context. This is how God intended the Scriptures to be to us, as a living letter. If you have a concordance, feel free to look up related verses and study the verses that are used even further.

1. Read John Chapter 15 as a whole, trying to understand it as one full analogy, with its intentions and insinuations.
2. Can you think of another analogy other than the vine, its branches, and its fruit that would symbolize the union of Christian and Jesus?
3. Galatians 4:6 holds a very key element of this

relationship for us to grasp. What is it? Does this change your view of the vine/branch arrangement?
4. All the Vine has is for the branch. What does this mean? What does Jesus, the Vine, have for us?
5. All that the branch has is for the vine. What is the significance of this for us? What do we have for the Lord?

5

YOU CAME TO CHRIST BY FAITH

"Therefore, as you received Christ Jesus the Lord, so walk in him, rooted and built up in him and established in the faith, just as you were taught, abounding in thanksgiving."
–Colossians 2:6-7

Paul teaches us an important lesson in this verse: Not only do we come to Jesus and be united to Him in faith, but by faith, we are to be rooted and established in our relationship with Jesus. As crucial as it is for the start, faith is vital for the rest of our spiritual lives. Abiding in Jesus can only be by faith.

There are sincere Christians who don't understand this, or they fail to realize how it works in practice. They are excited about the free gift of accepting Christ and being justified by faith. But then they think everything after that depends on hard work and commitment. While they understand that the sinner will be justified by faith, they haven't comprehended the bigger truth of living by faith. They haven't understood that Jesus is a perfect savior—He will do as much for them today as He did the first day when they came to Him. They don't know that the life of grace is living in faith. In a relationship with Jesus, the one duty of a Christian is to believe, because believing is the channel that grace and strength can flow into the heart of man.

The Christian's old nature is still evil and sinful. It's only as we come empty and helpless to our Savior to receive His life and strength, that we can bear fruits of righteousness. *"Therefore, as you received Christ Jesus the Lord, so walk in him, rooted and built up in him and established in the faith, just as you were taught, abounding in thanksgiving."* As you came to Jesus, so abide in Him, by faith.

To know how faith is used in abiding in Jesus, to be more deeply and firmly rooted in Him, you only have to look back to when first you received Him. You'll remember the obstacles that stopped you from believing. Your wickedness and guilt: It seemed impossible that forgiveness and love could be for such a sinner. Weakness and death: you had no power to surrender and trust. The future: You couldn't be a disciple of Jesus knowing you would fall again and again.

These were like mountains in your way. And how were they removed? Simply by the word of God. That word compelled you to believe that, despite the past guilt, present weakness, and future unfaithfulness, the promise that Jesus would accept and save you was solid. On that word you came and were not deceived. You found that Jesus did accept and save.

Your experience in coming to Jesus is similar to abiding in Him. There are many temptations to keep you from believing. You're filled with shame thinking of your sins since you became a Christian, and it feels like Jesus won't accept you into His love. When you think about how you have failed in the past, your present weakness makes you tremble to even say, "From now on, I will abide in You." And when you accept the life of love, joy, holiness, and fruitfulness, which in the future will flow from abiding in Him, it only makes you feel more hopeless. You can never achieve it. You know yourself too well. It's no use expecting it, only to be disappointed; a life completely abiding in Jesus is not for you.

But learn the lesson from when you first came to Jesus! Remember that despite your experience, feelings, and intelligence, you took Jesus at His word, and you were not disappointed. He received, pardoned, loved, and saved you. If He did this for you when you were an enemy and a stranger, how much more will He fulfill His promise now that you belong to Him? Does He really mean that I should abide in Him? The answer His word gives is so simple and so sure: By His grace, you now are in Him, and that same grace will enable you to abide in Him. By faith, you entered grace; by that same faith, you can enjoy the continuous grace of abiding in Him.

What must you believe in order to abide in Him? Believe that He says: "*I am the Vine.*" The safety and fruitfulness of the branch depend on the strength of the vine. Don't think of yourself as a branch, nor of the duty of abiding, until your heart is filled with faith that Christ is the Vine. He will be everything that a vine can be—holding you, nourishing you, and taking responsibility for your growth and your fruit.

Take time to know and believe: My Vine, on whom I can depend for everything, is Christ. A large, strong vine bears the weak branch and holds it more than the branch holds the vine. Ask the Father by the Holy Spirit to reveal to you what a glorious, loving, mighty Christ your life is in. It's faith in what Christ is that will keep you abiding in Him. A heart thinking of the Vine will be a strong branch and will abide confidently in Him. Occupy yourself with Jesus, and believe in Him as the True Vine.

Once you have the faith to say, "He is my Vine," then you can say, "I am His branch, I am in Him." I cannot say how important it is to exercise your faith by saying, "I am in Him." It makes the abiding so simple. Once I realize that I am in Him, I see that there is nothing left but my agreement to be what He has made me, to remain where He has put me.

I am in Christ: This simple thought, carefully, prayerfully, believingly said, removes all difficulty of trying to achieve something great. I am in Christ, my blessed Savior. His love has prepared a home for me with Him, when He says, "Abide in my love." His power will keep me if I just let Him. I am in Christ: I only have to say, "Savior, thank You for this wonderful grace. I surrender myself to You. I do abide in You."

It's amazing how faith like this works out everything in abiding in Christ. Christians need prayer, self-denial, obedience, and commitment, but "*all things are possible for one who believes*" (Mark 9:23). "*This is the victory that has overcome the world—our faith*" (1 John 5:4). It's faith that turns a blind eye to our weakness and finds joy in the sufficiency of an Almighty Savior, that makes the heart strong and glad. It gives itself up to be led by the Holy Spirit into a deeper appreciation of the wonderful Savior God has given us— Infinite Emmanuel.

Faith follows as the Spirit leads us through the Bible to reveal Jesus and His promises of nourishment and life. In line with the promise, "*If what you heard from the beginning abides in you, then you too will abide in the Son and in the Father,*" it lives by every word that comes from God (1 John 2:24). So, it strengthens the heart with the strength of God, to be and do all that is needed for abiding in Christ.

If you will abide in Christ: Only believe. Believe always; believe now. Bow before your Lord, and say to Him in childlike faith, that because He is your Vine, and you are His branch, you will abide in Him today.

Note

"I am the True Vine." He who offers us the privilege of an actual union with Himself is the great I AM, the almighty God, who upholds all things by the word of His power. And this almighty God reveals Himself as our perfect Savior, even so far as renewing our fallen natures by grafting them into His own Divine nature.

To realize the glorious Deity of Him whose call sounds forth to longing hearts with such exceeding sweetness is no small step towards gaining the full privilege to which we are invited. But longing is useless by itself; even less can we profit from reading the results to be gained from a close and personal union with our Lord, if we believe that union to be practically beyond our reach.

His words are meant to be a living, eternal, marvelous reality. And this they can never become unless we are sure that we may reasonably expect their accomplishment. But what could make the accomplishment of such an idea possible—what could make it reasonable to suppose that we poor, weak, selfish creatures, full of sin and full of failures, might be saved out of the corruption of our nature and made partakers of the holiness of our Lord—except the fact, the marvelous, unalterable fact, that He who proposes to us so great a transformation is Himself the everlasting God, as able as He is willing to fulfill His own word.

In meditating, therefore, upon these utterances of Christ, containing as they do the very essence of His teaching, the very concentration of His love, let us, at the outset, put away all tendency to doubt. Let us not allow ourselves so much as to question whether such erring disciples as we are can be enabled to attain the holiness to which we are called through a close and intimate union with our Lord. If there be any impossibility, any falling short of the proposed blessedness, it will arise from the lack of earnest desire on our part. There is no lack in any respect on His part who puts forth the invitation; with GOD there can be no shortcoming in the fulfillment of His promise. –*The Life of Fellowship; Meditations on John 15:1,11* by A. M. James.

. . .

For the sake of young or doubting Christians, there is something more necessary than exercising faith in each promise that is brought to our attention. What is of even more importance is the cultivation of trust towards God, the habit of always thinking of Him, His ways, and His works, with confident hopefulness.

Only in this type of soil do the individual promises take root and grow up. In a little work published by the Tract Society, *Encouragements to Faith*, by James Kimball, we can find many suggestions and helpful thoughts, all about why God has the right to be trusted.

The Christian's Secret of a Happy Life is another little work that has been very helpful to many. Its bright and easy tone, its loving repetition of the keynote—we may depend on Jesus to do all He has said, and more than we can think—has breathed hope and joy into many hearts that were almost ready to give up on ever getting anywhere. In Frances Havergal's *Kept for the Master's Use*, there is the same healthful, hope-inspiring tone.

STUDY GUIDE

As you will see in the Note at the end of this chapter, Murray was always looking for books and text that will corroborate and broaden his understanding of things like Faith. Don't be afraid of consulting other reputable sources, or even a concordance, to give you a better chance to grasp some of the deeper spiritual aspects. Allow these study questions to foster a curiosity to understand God and His Word more and more.

1. What is Faith? (see Hebrews 11:1) Is it the same thing as believing?
2. What roles does it play in our relationship as the branch to the Vine?
3. Look at this phrase used in the chapter, "...despite your experience, feelings, and intelligence..." Do you think this has any connection with having faith?
4. What does Murray say we need to believe in order to abide in Jesus?
5. Look at Roman 1:17, Galatians 3:11, and Hebrews 10:38. The same phrase is repeated. What does this mean in the context of the chapter you have just read?
6. If you haven't already noticed, the phrase is a quote taken from the Old Testament: Habakkuk 2:4. Do you see the same meaning here?
7. The great I AM that upholds all things, calls us to this relationship. What does this mean for us?

6

GOD HAS UNITED YOU TO CHRIST

"And because of him you are in Christ Jesus, who became to us wisdom from God, righteousness and sanctification and redemption."
–1 Corinthians 1:30

"My Father is the vinedresser."
–John 15:1

"You *are* in Christ Jesus." The believers at Corinth were still new, weak Christians. Paul wanted them to know that they were in Jesus. The whole Christian life depends on understanding our position in Christ. To abide in Christ, we need to be reminded that "I am in Christ Jesus." All powerful, fruitful sermons should begin with "*You are in Christ Jesus.*"

But Paul adds a more important phrase: "**Because of him** *you are in Christ Jesus.*" He wants us to remember our union with Jesus, but that it's not because we have done anything, but the work of God Himself. As the Holy Spirit helps us to realize this, we will see how much of a promise and strength it is for us. If it's because of God that I am in Jesus, then He becomes my security for all I need to abide in Christ.

Let us understand properly what this means: "**Because of him** *you are in Christ Jesus.*" In being united with Christ, there is a work God does and a work we have to do. God does His work by motivating us to do our work. The work of God is hidden and silent. What we do is something specific and physical. Conversion, faith, prayer, and obedience are all conscious acts we can identify. But spiritual inspiration and strengthening that come from above are secret and beyond what we can see or determine.

Often, we say, "I am in Christ Jesus," and look at what we have done, rather than all that God has done to unite us to Christ. It is good to say, "I know that I have believed." But we need to see that in our turning, believing, and accepting of Christ, God's power was very busy. He inspired us, took hold of us, and carried out His purpose in bringing us into Jesus. When we realize the divine aspect of our salvation, we will begin to praise and worship with grateful hearts. We will see that it is because of God.

Understanding this will open our hearts and minds to understand eternity. "*Those whom he predestined he also called*" (Rom 8:30). he called us because He has a plan for us in eternity. Before the world was made, God's love and grace chose us in Christ. Knowing that you are in Christ, is the stepping-stone to understanding the full meaning of "*Because of him you are in Christ Jesus.*"

As the prophet said, so you will also be able to say, "*The Lord appeared to him from afar. I have loved you with an everlasting love; therefore I have continued my faithfulness to you*" (Jer. 31:3). You will recognize your salvation as a part of that "*mystery of his will, according to his purpose which he set forth in Christ,*" and then be able to say, "*in him, according to the purpose of him who accomplishes all things according to the counsel of his will*" (Eph. 1:11) Nothing else will lift grace to its rightful place, and bring us to bow before it, than knowing the mystery of: "*Because of him you are in Christ Jesus.*"

It's easy to see how this will change our view of abiding in Christ. What a strong foundation we will have to surrender to Jesus than knowing the Father's purpose and work! We have thought of Christ as the Vine and the believer as the branch. But we must not forget that "*My Father is the vinedresser.*"

Jesus said, "*Every plant which my heavenly Father has not planted will be rooted up.*" But every branch grafted by Him in the True Vine, shall never be taken out of His hand. Jesus owed all that He was to the Father, His strength, and His life as the Vine. So, we owe our place and security in Christ to the Father. The same love and delight with which the Father watched over His Son, watches over everyone who is in Christ Jesus.

What a confident trust this faith inspires. Not only are we kept safely to the end, but to fulfill in us everything that we have been united to Christ for. The vinedresser is just as concerned with the growth of the vine as he is with the branch. The God who chose Christ to be Vine gave Him everything He needed to be the Vine. The God who has chosen and planted me in Christ has made me worthy of being in Jesus.

What confidence and urgency this gives to my prayers! How it inspires my dependence on Him and makes me see that praying without ceasing is the one need of my life—an unceasing waiting on the God who has united me to Christ, to perfect His own divine work in me according to His pleasure.

What a motivation this will bring in living a fruitful life! Clear and worthy motives are powerful, especially one that says, *"For we are his workmanship, created in Christ Jesus for good works"* (Eph. 2:10). Whatever God creates is exquisitely suited to its end. He created the sun to give light; it works perfectly! He created the eye to see; it performs beautifully! He created the Christian to do good works; it is our worthiest purpose.

Because of Him, I am a new creation, a branch of the Vine, made to bear fruit. We need to stop looking at our old natures, and complaining of our weaknesses as if God called us to something He could not accomplish! We should joyfully accept the revelation of God uniting us to Christ, and making Himself in charge of our spiritual growth and fruitfulness! Our laziness and doubt will disappear if we have this motivation. Trusting in the faithfulness of God, everything in us will rise to accept and fulfill our glorious destiny!

I surrender my heart to the mighty influence of this word: "*Because of him you are in Christ Jesus.*" It is the same God who made Christ to be everything for us, that we can be in Christ, and can be made to be what He designed us to be. Take time to meditate and worship, until God's light shines in you, to reveal your union to Christ as the work of His almighty Father. Take time every day, with all your work, needs, and wants, to let God be everything.

As Jesus says, "Abide in me," see Him pointing upward, saying, "My Father is the vinedresser. Because of Him, you are in me, through Him you abide in me, and to Him and His glory you will bear fruit." Let your answer be, Amen, Lord! So be it. From eternity, Christ and I were predestined for each other; we belong to each other. It is God's will. I shall abide in Christ. It is because of God that I am in Christ Jesus.

STUDY GUIDE

If you've made it this far without skipping a day, you've done well. If not, don't give up. Keep going. Some of the topics may even need extra reflection and time to sink in before rushing into the next chapter. Rather, let the Holy Spirit reveal things to you than trying your hardest to stick to a schedule and finish it. There is much to learn, and taking your time is far better than completing the journey without seeing anything along the way.

1. It will be good to understand the full meaning of the word, 'because' and the effects it has on understanding the key verse of this chapter.

2. This chapter begins to separate and see what is God's work, and what is our work. Making two columns and listing these as Murray states them will be an excellent exercise. It will make it very clear.
3. Look at Ephesians 1:11 and Romans 8:29-30. What does the word 'predestined' mean? How does this change our view on what we have done and what God has done?
4. What is the vinedresser's role in the picture of the vine and branches? Who is the vinedresser and what does He do in our relationship with Jesus?
5. What is the relationship of God, the Father, and His Son, Jesus? (see John 10:30)
6. What do you make of the statement that God has not "called us to something He could not accomplish?"

7

CHRIST AS YOUR WISDOM

*"And because of him you are in Christ Jesus, who became to us **wisdom** from God, righteousness and sanctification and redemption."*
−1 Corinthians 1:30

Jesus is not only a Priest to purchase and a King to secure, but also a Prophet to reveal to us the salvation God has prepared for those that love Him. Just as he first called light into existence so that we could appreciate the life and beauty of His creation, wisdom is mentioned in this verse as the place we will find three precious gifts. Life is the light of man; revealing the glory of God so we can enter eternal life through Jesus. The tree of knowledge revealed sin; salvation comes through the knowledge Jesus gives us. God made Him to be wisdom for us. In Him, all the treasures of wisdom and knowledge are hidden.

Because of God, you are in Him and can abide in Him, to enjoy these treasures of wisdom. We are in Him, and wisdom is in Him. Living in Him, you live in the fountain of all light. Abiding in Him, you have Jesus, the wisdom of God, leading your whole spiritual life, ready to give you all the knowledge you require. Jesus is wisdom to us: We are in Jesus.

We need to understand our union with Jesus, and what it brings to us, better. The blessings in Christ are not gifts given because we have prayed for them but are ours because we are abiding in Him. These prayers are answered as our union with Him and abiding in Him grow deeper. All the gifts contained in wisdom and knowledge are ours.

Have you longed for wisdom and spiritual understanding to know God better? Abide in Jesus: It will lead you to fellowship with God where you will find the knowledge of God. His love, power, and glory will be revealed beyond what we are able to imagine. You might not understand it with your mind or to express it in words; but the knowledge which is deeper than thoughts or words will be given—knowing God which comes from being known of Him. *"We preach Christ crucified...to those who are called...Christ the power of God and the wisdom of God"* (1 Cor 1:23-24).

Would you like to count everything as a loss compared to the excellence of knowing Jesus (Phil 3:8)? Abide in Jesus, and be found in Him. You will know Him in the power of His resurrection and the fellowship of His sufferings (Phil 3:10). Following Him, you won't walk in darkness, but have the light of life. It is only when God shines into your heart, and

Jesus lives there, that the light of the knowledge of God in the face of Christ can be seen.

Would you like to understand what He has done on earth and heaven by His Spirit? Would you like to know how Christ can become our righteousness, sanctification, and redemption? As these are revealed to us, He becomes the wisdom of God.

Often, we have a thousand questions that are just too much to try and answer. It's because you have forgotten you are in Christ, whom God has made to be your wisdom. Your first priority should be to abide in Him with all your heart. When your heart and life are rooted in Jesus, knowledge will come as He sees fit to give you. Without abiding in Christ, knowledge is useless, even damaging. Too many times, we are satisfied with thoughts that we think are true, but they lack the power of real truth.

The way God works is to give us a seed, life, and power, then knowledge. We look for knowledge first and never go any further. God gives us Jesus, and in Him are all the treasures of wisdom and knowledge. We must be content with Jesus, to live in Him, make Him our life, and as we search deeper into Him, we will find the knowledge we desire. This knowledge is life.

So, abide in Jesus as your wisdom, and expect whatever teaching you may need for a life that glorifies the Father. In your spiritual life, abide in Jesus as your wisdom. The life you have in Christ is too high and holy for you to know how to act it out. Only He can guide you in the Spirit to know how to mature as a child of God, what will help or block your heart, and especially abiding in Him. Don't think it's a mystery or problem you must solve.

Whatever questions you have about how to properly abide in Him, and receive all the blessings, just remember: He knows. Everything is clear to Him, and He is your wisdom. He will give you all the knowledge and ability if you only trust Him. Don't think that all the treasures of wisdom and knowledge in Jesus have no key or your path has no light. Jesus is the wisdom that guides you.

In all your reading of the Bible, remember the truth: Abide in Jesus, He is your wisdom. Study the Bible as much as you can, but study the living Word more. Jesus, the wisdom of God, can only be found through confidence and obedience. The words He speaks are spirit and life to those who live in Him. Every time you read, hear or meditate on the Bible, remember your priority. Realize your oneness with Jesus, the wisdom of God; know you are under His direct and special training; go to the Bible as you abide in Him, the fountain of divine light—in His light, you shall see light.

In your daily life and work, abide in Jesus as your wisdom, he will guide you. Your body is His temple and your daily life is the place to glorify Him. He is concerned that you are guided correctly through all your choices. Trust His sympathy, believe His love, and wait for His guidance—it will be given. Abiding in Him, the mind will be calm and free from passion, your judgment clear and strong. The light of heaven will shine on earthly things, and just like Solomon's prayer for wisdom, you will be given whatever you ask or think.

More than your everyday work, abide in Jesus as your wisdom when going about the Lord's work. "*For we are his workmanship, created in Christ Jesus for good works, which God prepared beforehand, that we should walk in them*" (Eph 2:10). Let every fear and doubt be put aside. In Christ we are created to do His works, He will show us what they are, and how to do them. Grow in the habit knowing that divine wisdom is guiding you, even when you can't see the way before you.

All you want to know is perfectly clear to Him. As Man and Mediator, He has access to the Father, to the secrets of Providence, on your behalf. If you will trust Him completely, and abide in Him, you can be confident of having guidance that never fails.

Abide in Jesus as your wisdom. Have a spirit that is used to waiting and depending on Him, always learning and never moving unless He leads you. Block out all the distractions, don't listen to the world, and be a student that listens to all wisdom the Master has to teach. Surrender your own wisdom. Understand that your natural understanding cannot find the things of God. Whatever you believe and do, wait for Jesus to teach and to guide you.

Remember that teaching and guidance don't come from other places outside of Jesus. His life in us is where divine wisdom works. Take time to be alone with Him in your heart, where the gentle voice of the Spirit can only be heard if everything is still. Be confident, even in dark times and when you feel alone, that He is the light and will lead you.

Every day, live in the truth that, as Jesus is your wisdom, your only priority is to abide in Him. When you abide in Him, His wisdom will spontaneously come to you, as your life is rooted in Him. As you abide in Christ, who is our wisdom from God, wisdom will be given to you.

STUDY GUIDE

As before, the purpose and encouragement of these study questions are to move you into a deeper understanding and desire to know more of Him. If you have a different translation of the Bible, don't be confused. In fact, this can often be more helpful as certain words appear in different versions and can be easier to understand or give clarification. The New King James Version, the New American Standard Bible, the New International Version, and New Living Translation, even the English Revised Version, are some options. Either way, having a Bible close by is crucial for spiritual growth.

1. What is wisdom? Look at James 3:13-18 to see the difference between worldly and Godly wisdom.
2. In the key verse, 1 Cor 1:30, wisdom is not one of the gifts, but the actual place we find them. Why do you think this is?
3. Why do you think we are often obsessed with having knowledge and knowing something? What is the danger of this? Look at 1 Cor 8:1.
4. What is the difference between knowing about Him and knowing Him?
5. What do you understand by this statement: "The way

God works is to give us a seed, life, and power, then knowledge?"
6. Murray suggests surrendering your own wisdom, your natural understanding, everything you believe and do. How easy is this for you to do?

8

CHRIST AS YOUR RIGHTEOUSNESS

*"And because of him you are in Christ Jesus, who became to us wisdom from God, **righteousness** and sanctification and redemption."*
–1 Corinthians 1:30

The first blessing that Christ, our wisdom, reveals to us is righteousness. It's not difficult to see why this is first.

No nation, home, or heart can prosper or grow unless there is peace. A machine can't even do its work unless it rests or is properly secured, so our moral and spiritual lives can't function correctly without peace and stability.

Sin turned everything upside down; we were out of harmony with ourselves, with men, and with God. The first requirement of salvation was peace, and this can only come when things are right. When everything is in order with the way God created it to be, and in line with His will, then peace can reign. Jesus came to restore peace on earth and in our hearts by restoring righteousness.

In the Bible, He is called Melchizedek, King of righteousness, and so He reigns as King of Salem, King of peace (Heb.7:2). He fulfills the promise of the prophets: "*A king will reign in righteousness: And the effect of righteousness will be peace, and the result of righteousness, quietness and trust forever*" (Isa.32:1,17). God has made Jesus our righteousness; because of God we are in Him as our righteousness; we are made the righteousness of God in Him. Let's try to understand what this means.

When a sinner comes to trust in Christ for salvation, they look to what He has done and will do, more than who He is.

As they look at the cross, and the Righteous One suffering for the unrighteous, they see God's forgiving mercy. Jesus as the substitute, taking on their curse, and dying in their place, the sinner finds peace. And as they understand how He brings righteousness to be theirs, and that they are now counted as righteous before God, they are restored to favor with God: "*We have been justified by faith, we have peace with God*" (Rom 5:1). It's as if they are dressed in righteousness in the faith of this gift that has been given to them.

As new Christians, they now want to understand how God justifies sinners on the strength of the righteousness of another. The answer is found in the relationship of the believer with Jesus as the second Adam. Because Christ made

Himself one with His people, and they were one with Him; each member of the body could now benefit from the head's actions and sufferings. It becomes clear that only through a personal relationship with Christ as the Head, can the power of His righteousness bring them into favor and fellowship with the Holy One. Jesus' work doesn't lose its importance but leads their hearts to a deeper love of who He is to them.

This reveals more verses: How the righteousness of God, as it becomes ours, is connected with the Redeemer.

- "*And this is the name by which he will be called: 'The Lord is our righteousness'*" (Jer 23:6).
- "*Only in the Lord, it shall be said of me, are righteousness and strength*" (Isa 45:24).
- "*Because of him...Christ Jesus...became to us... righteousness*" (1 Cor 1:30).
- "*That in him we might become the righteousness of God*" (2 Cor 5:21).
- "*Be found in him, not having a righteousness of my own, but...the righteousness from God*" (Phil 3:9).

It becomes clear how connected righteousness and Jesus' life are to each other:

- "*One act of righteousness leads to justification and life for all men*" (Rom 5:18).
- "*Those who receive...the free gift of righteousness reign in life through the one man Jesus Christ*" (Rom 5:17).

The deep meaning of the key-word in Romans becomes very clear:

- "*The righteous shall live by faith*" (Rom 1:17).

Being dressed in righteousness is not enough, they would rather put on Jesus, and be clothed with Himself and His life —the righteousness of God is theirs because the Lord, our righteousness, is theirs. Before understanding this, it was difficult to wear righteous clothes all day. It was as if they had to dress up every time they came into God's presence to confess sins and find grace. But now Jesus is their righteousness—the One who watches over, and keeps and loves us as His own; it's not impossible anymore to walk the whole day dressed in the loving presence with which He covers His people.

This reveals even more. Life and righteousness are linked, and the believer becomes conscious of a righteous nature planted within them. The new man created in Christ Jesus is "*created after the likeness of God in true righteousness and holiness*" (Eph 4:24). "*Whoever practices righteousness is righteous, as he is righteous*" (1 John 3:7). The union with Jesus hasn't just brought a change in the relation to God, but also in the personal state before God. As this fellowship is maintained, righteousness becomes their very nature.

To Christians that begin to see the deep meaning of Jesus being made righteousness to us, it's hardly necessary to say "Abide in Him." Only seeing the righteousness of the substitute, and how we are counted righteous for His sake, the need to abide in Him is not clear. But as the glory of the

Lord our righteousness is revealed, abiding in Him personally is the only way to stand before God, complete and accepted. It's the only way to realize how our new and righteous nature can be strengthened from Jesus our Head. To the repentant sinner, the main thought was righteousness through Jesus dying for sin; to the intelligent and growing Christian, Jesus, through whom righteousness comes, is everything, because having Him he has the righteousness too.

Abide in Christ as your righteousness. You carry a nature that's corrupt and evil, always trying to rise up and convince you that you have no right and no access to fellowship with the Father. Nothing can enable you to live and walk in the light of God, but abiding in Jesus as your righteousness. This is what you are called to. Live worthy of that calling.

Allow the Holy Spirit to reveal to you the wonderful grace that lets you come to God, dressed in divine righteousness. Realize that it's the King's robe that has been put on you and that you don't need to fear entering His presence as you wear it. It's a sign that you are someone the King delights to honor. Remember that as much as you need it in the palace, you also require it when He sends you out into the world as the King's messenger and representative. Live your daily life conscious of being righteous in God's sight, a delight and pleasure in Christ. Every view you have of Jesus must first come from the fact that He has been made righteousness to you. This will keep you in perfect peace and you will enter and live in God's rest.

In this way, you will be transformed into being righteous and doing righteousness. It will show through your heart and life. As you abide in Jesus, the Righteous One, you will share His position and character: *"You have loved righteousness and hated wickedness; therefore God, your God, has anointed you with the oil of gladness beyond your companions"* (Heb 1:9). Joy and gladness will be yours.

STUDY GUIDE

In some books, you just have to stop and reread certain chapters. They hold such knowledge and information that is so deep, it takes us a few passes to actually recognize what we are looking at. These chapters revolving around 1 Corinthians 1:30 are really important to grasp. They also tackle aspects of Christianity that we take for granted but know very little about. If you have to read a chapter again, do it. Ask the Holy Spirit to open your eyes. And, as we read in the last chapter, let Him give you the wisdom to understand.

1. What is righteousness?
2. Murray makes a very interesting connection between peace and righteousness. What is it?
3. Who was Melchizedek? What is the connection to Jesus? Look at Genesis 14:18, Psalm 110:4, and Hebrews 5:5-6.
4. How do we receive righteousness? Is there something we have to do to achieve it?
5. How has Jesus been made righteousness to us?
6. Murray talks about being clothed in righteousness as

opposed to putting on righteous clothes every time. What is the difference?
7. How does the analogy of being a king's subject and wearing his robe as a sign of honor make righteousness clear for us?

9

CHRIST AS YOUR SANCTIFICATION

> *"And because of him you are in Christ Jesus, who became to us wisdom from God, righteousness and **sanctification** and redemption"*
> –1 Corinthians 1:30

The first chapter of 1 Corinthians starts in verse 2, teaching us that Christ is our sanctification: *"To the church of God that is in Corinth, to those sanctified in Christ Jesus, called to be saints."* In the Old Testament, believers were called the righteous; in the New Testament, they are called saints, the holy ones, sanctified in Christ Jesus. Holy is higher than righteous [1].

Holy in God refers to His nature. Righteous refers to His dealings with His people. For us, righteousness is a steppingstone to holiness; the way to get as close to the perfection of God as possible (See Matt. 5:48; I Pet. 1:16). In the Old Testament, righteousness was found, while holiness was only represented. In Jesus, the Holy One, and in His people, His saints or holy ones, it is now realized.

In the Bible, and in life, righteousness comes before holiness. When we first find Christ as our righteousness, it brings us so much joy that studying holiness hardly features. But as we grow, the desire for holiness grows, and we want to know how God has made a way for us to get there. A shallow understanding leads us to think that justification is God's work, by faith in Christ, but sanctification is our work, that we must perform because we are so thankful for having been delivered. If we are sincere, though, we see that just being grateful doesn't give us enough power. Even though prayer is vital, we find that it is also not enough. We can struggle like this for years, until we listen to the Spirit, as He glorifies and reveals Christ, who is our sanctification through faith alone.

God made Jesus to be our sanctification. Holiness is God's nature, and whatever He takes hold of and fills with Himself, will become holy. How can a sinful person become holy? God's answer is Jesus, "*the Holy One of God*" (John 6:69). The Father sanctified and sent Jesus into the world to reveal His holiness in physical form for us to see and understand.

"*And for their sake I consecrate myself, that they also may be sanctified in truth*" (John 17:19). There is no other way for us to become holy, except by sharing in the holiness of Jesus [2]. And there is no other way this can happen except through our relationship with Him so that the Holy Spirit can pour His holy life into us. "*Because of him you are in Christ Jesus, who became to us... sanctification.*"

Abiding in Christ our sanctification is the simple secret of a holy life. How holy we become, will depend on how much we abide in Him. As we learn to abide in Christ, the promise comes true: "*Now may the God of peace himself sanctify you completely*" (1 Thess 5:23).

To understand how the measure of abiding and the measure of sanctification relate to each other, we can look at how a tree is grafted, the picture of our union to Jesus. Jesus said, "*Make the tree good and its fruit good*" (Matt 12:33). I can graft a tree so that only one branch bears good fruit, while the natural branches still bear their old fruit. This is like a Christian who has a small part of their life sanctified, while the rest of it is still living for their own pleasures.

I can graft a tree so that every branch is cut off, and the whole tree is renewed to bear good fruit. But if I don't keep checking, the old stems can sprout, grow again, and suck the strength from the new graft, making it weak. These Christians are often radically born again, giving up everything to follow Jesus, but soon get slack and allow old habits back in, making their Christian life and fruit weak.

But if I want to make a tree fruitful, I cut the stem down to the ground when it's young, and graft it right where it comes up from the soil. I watch over every bud to make sure the old nature doesn't sprout, until the sap from the old roots flows so strongly into the new stem, that the old life has no chance and is completely taken over by the new. This is a renewed tree—a Christian who has learned to surrender everything to Jesus and abide in Him with complete faith.

If the gardener could talk to the tree, and the tree was willing to cooperate, he might say, "Surrender to this new nature that I have invested in you; squash every chance the old nature has to sprout; let all your sap and all your life flow into this graft that I have put on you; then you will bear lots of sweet fruit."

The tree would respond: "When you graft me, cut off every branch; Destroy everything of the old self, even the smallest bud, that I may no longer live that way, but rather in the grafted branch, where I can become new and good."

Once the renewed tree begins bearing abundant fruit, it would say: "Nothing good is in my roots. I always lean towards evil; the sap I draw from the soil is naturally corrupt and will show itself in bearing evil fruit. But just as the sap rises into the sunshine to ripen into fruit, the wise gardener has clothed me with a new life. Then my sap is purified. My power to bear good fruits renewed. I only have to abide in what I have received. He takes care of removing every old bud that wants to sprout."

Don't be afraid to take hold of God's promises to make you holy. Don't think that your old nature will make holiness impossible for you. There is nothing good in your flesh, and even though it is crucified with Christ, it is not completely dead, but will always try to rise and lead you to evil. But the Father is the vinedresser. He has grafted the life of Jesus on your life. That holy life is mightier than your evil life. Under the care of the vinedresser, that new life can squash the evil life inside you. The evil nature is there, but the new nature is there too—Jesus, your sanctification—and through Him, you can be sanctified, and be made to bear fruit to the glory of the Father.

If you would live a holy life, abide in Christ your sanctification. He is the Holy One of God, made man that He might show us the holiness of God. The Bible teaches us that in you, a new nature, a new man, was created in Jesus in righteousness and true holiness. Remember that this holy nature which is in you is made specifically for living a holy life, just as the old nature is for doing evil. Understand that this holy nature inside of you has its root and life in Jesus, and can only grow and become strong as the relationship is not broken.

Believe that Jesus delights in maintaining this new nature within you, and gives His own strength and wisdom to make it work. Let that faith lead you to surrender all your self-confidence every day and confess how naturally corrupt you are. Let it fill you with a quiet, strong confidence that you are able to do what the Father expects of you as His child because you have Christ strengthening you in grace.

Let it teach you to lay yourself and your works on the altar as spiritual sacrifices, holy and acceptable in His sight, a sweet fragrance to Him. Don't look at a life of holiness as a strain and an effort, but as the natural growth of Jesus in you. Let a still, hopeful, faith remind you that all you need for a holy life will be given to you from the holiness of Jesus. Then you will understand and show what it is to abide in Christ our sanctification.

Note

[1] "Holiness may be called spiritual perfection, as righteousness is legal completeness." –Horatius Bonar in *God's Way of Holiness*.

[2] The concept that in the holiness of our Lord a new holy nature was formed to be shown and taught to us, and that we make use of it by faith, is the central idea of Walter Marshall's invaluable work, *The Gospel Mystery of Sanctification*:

One great mystery is, that the holy frame and disposition whereby our souls are furnished and enabled for immediate practice of the law, must be obtained by receiving it out of Christ's fullness, as a thing already prepared and brought to existence for us in Christ, and treasured up in Him; and that, as we are justified by righteousness wrought out in Christ, and imputed to us, so we are sanctified by such a holy frame and qualification as are first wrought out and completed in Christ for us, and then imparted to us. As our natural corruption was produced originally in the first Adam, and propagated from him to us, so our new nature and holiness is first produced in Christ, and derived from Him to us, or, as it were, propagated. So that we are not at all to work together with Christ in making or producing that holy frame in us, but only to take it to ourselves, and use it in our holy practice, as made ready to our hands. Thus we have fellowship with Christ, in receiving that holy frame of spirit that was originally in Him; for fellowship is where several persons have the same things in common. This mystery is so great, that notwithstanding all the light of the Gospel, we commonly think that we must get a holy frame by producing it anew in ourselves, and by pursuing it and working it out of our own heart (see chap. 3).

I have felt so strongly that Marshall's teaching is exactly what the church needs to see what the biblical path of holiness is that I have prepared an abridgment of his work (all in the author's own words). By leaving out what was not essential to his argument, and shortening some longer parts, I hoped to bring his book to many who might never read the larger work. It's published by Nisbet & Co. as *The Highway of Holiness*. I can't stress enough for every student of theology, the Bible, and holy living, to study the teaching of the third, fourth, and twelfth chapters of this book.

STUDY GUIDE

If you are studying and discussing this in a group, you will be challenged by different viewpoints, humbled by the honesty of those admitting their lack and weakness in areas, and encouraged by others' desire to know more. Even though our spiritual growth depends on our individual relationship with Jesus, it is so helpful to have the input and opportunity to learn and grow with others. As much as possible, try and discuss points with other Christians—even those you look up to in the church.

1. What is sanctification? (see Hebrews 10:14)
2. Why does righteousness come before holiness?
3. Murray says that there is no other way to become holy but to share in Jesus' holiness. How does this happen?

4. 1 Peter 1:16 is a tall order when we read it as a command. What does it mean for you?
5. Are purification and sanctification the same thing? Look at 2 Corinthians 7:1 and 1 John 3:3 as you answer.
6. The excerpt in Note [2] makes this statement: "...we commonly think that we must get a holy frame by producing it anew in ourselves, and by pursuing it and working it out of our own heart." Have you ever felt like this? After reading this chapter on Sanctification, has your view changed?

CHRIST AS YOUR REDEMPTION

*"And because of him you are in Christ Jesus, who became to us wisdom from God, righteousness and sanctification and **redemption**."*
–1 Corinthians 1:30

This is like the top of the ladder that reaches into heaven—the wonderful end that Jesus and life in Him lead to.

Redemption is often used to describe deliverance from the guilt of sin. Here, it refers to our complete and final deliverance from all sin's consequences, when the Redeemer's work will be fully accomplished, even redemption of our bodies (see Rom. 8:21-23; Eph. 1.14; 4:30). It points us to the future glory we hope for, and the present blessing we can enjoy in Jesus.

As a Prophet, Christ is our wisdom, revealing God and His love in the salvation prepared for us. As a Priest, He is our righteousness, restoring our favor and friendship with God. As a King, He is our sanctification, guiding us into obedience to the Father's holy will. As these three work out God's one purpose of complete deliverance from sin, and ransomed humanity regaining all that it had ever lost.

God made Jesus to be our redemption. Here, we see Jesus as He lived on earth, teaching us by word and example, as He died, to reconcile us with God, as He lives again, a victorious King, rising to receive His crown. But we also see Him sitting at the right hand of God in the glory He first had with the Father, before the world began, and holds it there for us. His human nature in a physical body was set free from all sin's consequences He had to face and is now allowed to share in divine glory.

As Son of Man, He sits on the throne and in the presence of the Father: The deliverance from what He had to suffer from sin, is complete and eternal. Complete redemption is in His own Person: What He as man is, and has in heaven, is complete redemption. God made Him our redemption.

The more we abide in Him as our redemption, the more we will experience, even here, *"the powers of the age to come"* (Heb 6:5). As our relationship with Him becomes more intimate, and we let the Holy Spirit reveal Him to us in His heavenly glory, the more we realize the life in us is the life of One who sits upon the throne of heaven. We feel the power of an endless life working in us. We taste eternal life.

The blessings that flow from abiding in Christ as our redemption are incredible. The soul is delivered from all fear of death. Even Jesus feared death, but not anymore. He has triumphed over death; His body has entered into glory. The Christian that abides in Him as their redemption also has spiritual victory over death. It is now just a servant that removes the last rags of their physical bodies, to be dressed in a new body of glory. It carries the body to the grave, where the new body will rise as a glorified spirit. The resurrection of the body is not a forgotten belief, but a living expectation, because the Spirit of Him that raised Jesus from the dead, lives in the body as the promise of our physical bodies being renewed (Rom.8:11-23). The sanctification this faith brings comes from surrendering our sinful bodies to the Spirit, for the time when they will be changed into glorious ones.

This full redemption of Jesus that includes our bodies, is not easily understood. Humans were made in the image and likeness of God, soul, and body. Angels were created as spirits without physical bodies; the world was made as matter without spirit. Humans were the highest example of all He made: A combination of matter and spirit in perfect harmony—the perfect union between God and His creation.

Sin entered to destroy that: The physical became dominant over the spiritual. The Word was made flesh, the divine was embodied in Jesus as a man, that redemption would be complete and perfect. Now, all of creation groans in pain, waiting to be delivered from its corruption into the freedom and glory as children of God. God's purpose will not be accomplished, and Christ's glory will not be fully manifested, until the body has been changed by the power of the spiritual life, and renewed as a vessel to show the glory of the Spirit. Then we'll understand that Jesus was made to be our redemption.

For now, we must learn that *"because of him...Christ Jesus, became to us ...redemption."* This isn't something that we can only realize in the future; to grow as Christians in abiding in Him, we must take hold of it for our lives now. We do this by learning to triumph over death. We do it by learning to look at Jesus as Lord of our body, allowing Him to consecrate us, and through faith (Mark 16:17-18), having victory over the control of sin in the body. We do this by learning to look at creation as part of Jesus' Kingdom, destined to be part of His redemption. We do it by allowing the promise of eternity to lift us to a life in the heavenly places, enlarging our hearts and views, anticipating all those things that were too impossible to understand, except in our hearts.

Abide in Christ as your redemption. Let this be the crown of your Christian life. Don't make it the first or only thing you seek in Jesus, but as a progression to where He wants to lead you. Abide in Christ as your redemption. You can only do this by having faith as you follow His steps. Abide in Him as your wisdom, the perfect revelation of all that God is and has for you. Let Him order your inner and outer life in humility, and He will reveal secrets to you of which other Christians know nothing. The wisdom will lead you into the mysteries of complete redemption.

Abide in Him as your righteousness, and live in the Father's favor and presence that His righteousness gives you access to. Rejoice in being reconciled to Him, and you will understand how it includes everything, waiting for full redemption; *"For in him all the fullness of God was pleased to dwell, and through him to reconcile to himself all things, whether on earth or in heaven"* (Col 1:19-20). Abide in Him as your sanctification. The experience of His power to make you holy in spirit, soul, and body, will inspire your faith in a holiness that will not stop until everything is brought to be holy before Him.

Abide in Him as your redemption, living as the heir of the future glory. And as you seek the full power of His saving grace, your heart will realize man's destiny in the universe, having everything subject to him. Then you will be equipped to live worthy of that high and heavenly calling.

STUDY GUIDE

Understanding these three elements of Christianity; righteousness, sanctification, and redemption, can be difficult. If you have time to dive in deeper, then try reading a few other expositions on this subject. But as always, ask the Holy Spirit for guidance. It will be a futile experience to simply know about them, rather than to be enlightened and have a revelation in your heart of what they are to you.

Christ, the Believer's Wisdom, Righteousness, Sanctification and Redemption is a very good place to start. It's a collection of expositions and sermons on 1 Corinthians 1:30 by Charles Spurgeon, George Whitefield, Jonathan Edwards, Charles Hodge, John Calvin, and John Gill.

1. What is redemption? (see Ephesians 1:7) It will also

help to look up the meaning of the word redeem and redemption to understand its implications.
2. Why is redemption necessary?
3. What is the difference between "deliverance from the guilt of sin" and "deliverance from all sin's consequences?"
4. What is the redemption of our bodies? When does this occur?
5. How are eternity and redemption connected?
6. Murray cautions not to "make it the first or only thing you seek in Jesus," but rather a development of our lives in Christ. Why?
7. Now that you have read chapters 7 to 10, what is your conclusion of Wisdom that unlocks these three treasures of Jesus for us?

CHRIST THE CRUCIFIED ONE

"I have been crucified with Christ. It is no longer I who live, but Christ who lives in me."
–Galatians 2:20

"For if we have been united with him in a death like his."
–Romans 6:5

"**I have** been crucified with Christ." Paul is certain of his fellowship with Christ in His sufferings and death, and in all the power and the blessing of that death. Did he mean what he said, and know he was already dead, by adding: "*It is no longer I who live, but Christ who lives in me?*" What a blessing this type of relationship with Jesus must be! To be able to look on His death as mine—His perfect obedience to God, His victory over sin, and complete deliverance from its power. Then realize that the power of that death works in crucifying the flesh every day, renewing the whole life into the conformity of Jesus' resurrection life! Abiding in Jesus, the Crucified One, is the secret of that new life growing, despite being dead in nature.

"United with him in a death like his," teaches us what abiding in the Crucified One means. When a graft is united with the stem on which it will grow, we know it must be secured, it must abide in the place where the stem has been cut and wounded, to make an opening to receive the graft. There can be no graft without wounding—opening and exposing the inner life of the tree to receive the foreign branch. It is only through wounding that access to the sap, growth, and life of the stronger stem can be obtained.

It's the same with Jesus and the sinner. Only when we are planted into the likeness of His death can we be in the likeness of His resurrection, receiving the life and power in Him. On the cross, Jesus' opened wounds became a place in which we can be grafted. The same way you would say to the grafted branch, "Abide in the wound of the stem that will bear you;" so we can say to the Christian, "Abide in the wounds of Jesus; this where you'll find union, life, and growth. You'll see how His heart was opened to receive you; how His flesh was torn to open a way for you to be made one with Him and allow access to all the blessings that flow from Him."

It's also true that the graft has to be removed from the tree it first grew from, and be cut to prepare it to be placed in the wounded stem. The Christian also must be made to fit in Christ's death—to be crucified and to die with Him. The wounded stem and the wounded graft are cut to fit into each other's likeness. There is a fellowship between Christ's sufferings and your sufferings. His experiences must become yours. The manner in which He chose and bore the cross must be yours.

Like Him, you will have to agree to the righteous judgment of a holy God against sin. Like Him, you have to surrender your sinful, cursed life to death to be able to pass to new life. Like Him, you will experience that it's only through the self-sacrifice of Gethsemane and Calvary that the path to joy and bearing resurrection—life fruit can be found. The clearer the resemblance between the wounded stem and the wounded graft, the more exactly their wounds fit into each other, the easier and more complete the union and growth will be.

It's in Jesus, the Crucified One, I must abide. I mustn't look on the cross just as an atonement to God, but also as a victory over the devil—deliverance from guilt, as well as from the power of sin. His death on the cross must be mine, offering Himself to receive me into the closest fellowship, so that I can enter into the power of His death to sin, and the new life of victory. I must yield myself to Him in complete surrender, with prayer and a strong desire to enter a deeper conformity of His death, in the Spirit in which He died that death.

Why is the cross the place of union? On the cross, the Son of God enters into the fullest union with man—the fullest experience of a member of a race under the curse. In death, the Prince of life conquers the power of death; in death, He can bring me into that victory. The life He gives is a life from the dead; each new experience of the power of that life depends on the fellowship of the death. You cannot separate this death and life.

The grace Jesus gives is through the fellowship with Jesus the Crucified One. Christ came and took my place; I must put myself in His place, and abide there. There is only one place we share—the cross. It's His through the free choice he made to accept it. It's mine because of the curse of sin. He went to the cross to seek me; only there can I find Him. When He found me there, it was a cursed place, as it says, *"Cursed is everyone who is hanged on a tree"* (Gal 3:13). He turned it into a place of blessing because I was delivered from the curse when He became the curse for me.

When Jesus takes my place, He is still the Father's beloved Son, but in fellowship with me, He shares my curse and dies my death. When I stand in His place, I am still the condemned one that deserves to die, but united to Him, I receive His blessing and life. When He came to be one with me He couldn't avoid the cross, for the curse always points to the cross as its end and fruit. And when I seek to be one with Him, I can't avoid the cross either, for only on the cross are life and deliverance found.

As my curse pointed Him to the cross as the only place where He could be fully united to me, His blessing points me to the cross as the only place where I can be united to Him. He took my cross for His own. I must take His cross as my own. I must be crucified with Him. As I abide daily, deeply in the Crucified One, I will taste His sweet love, His powerful life, and His complete salvation.

The cross of Christ is a deep mystery. Unfortunately, many Christians are happy accepting Jesus dying on the cross for their sins, with no desire for fellowship with the Crucified One. They don't even know He invites them to it. Or maybe they think that their everyday sufferings are what it means to share in the cross. They have no idea what it means to be crucified with Christ—bearing the cross is identifying with Christ in His path of obedience.

Surrendering all of your will, denying your flesh's desires and pleasures, separating yourself from the world's ways of thinking and acting, losing and hating your life, giving up your interests for the sake of others—this is the character of someone that has taken up Christ's cross and says, "I am crucified with Christ; I abide in Christ, the Crucified One."

Do you want to please the Lord, and live in close fellowship with Him? Then pray that His Spirit shows you this secret. We know how Peter knew and confessed Jesus as the Son of the living God while the cross was still an offense (Matt. 16:16,17,21,23). The faith that believes in the forgiving blood, and the life that renews, can only grow as it abides in the cross, and in living fellowship with Him, conformed to Jesus the Crucified.

Jesus, our crucified Redeemer, teaches us not to just believe in You, but to abide in You, and take Your cross not only for our forgiveness but also as the law of our life. Teach us to love it not only because there You took our curse, but also because there we enter into the closest fellowship and are crucified with You. And teach us, that as we surrender ourselves to the Spirit in which You suffered the cross, we shall be joined to the power and the blessing that only the cross alone can access.

STUDY GUIDE

Concentrating on Jesus, crucified for us, we can become sentimental or even feel guilty because of what He went through on our behalf. We can even gloss over it and head straight on to rejoicing. But understanding what He did and why He did it, and what it means for us on a daily basis, is one of the key revelations of being a Christian. Let the questions help you find a deeper understanding of Jesus as the Crucified One.

1. What does Paul mean in saying, "I have been crucified with Christ?"
2. What does Murray mean by saying that we need to abide in Jesus' wounds?
3. How is it possible that the cross and Jesus' sufferings can become ours?
4. What is the connection between surrendering your will and being crucified with Christ?
5. Paul summed up his entire ministry by saying that he wanted to know nothing except "Christ and Him crucified" (1 Cor 2:2). What does this mean?
6. Would this be the statement that sums up your Christian life? Why?

GOD WILL ESTABLISH YOU IN CHRIST

> *"And it is God who establishes us with you in Christ."*
> –2 Corinthians 1:21

Paul teaches that the same way it was God who united us with Christ, so we must look to the Father to be kept in Him. "*The Lord will fulfill his purpose for me*" is a confident statement that should always end with the prayer, "*Do not forsake the work of your hands*" (Psalm 138:8). As Christians we must be confident in our desire and prayer to abide in Jesus deeper: "*He who began a good work in you will bring it to completion at the day of Jesus Christ*" (Phil 1:6). Nothing else will root us in Christ as this faith: "*It is God who establishes us with you in Christ.*"

This is the faith we need! Sometimes our spiritual life can be up and down. We can have moments where our hearts seek and experience God's grace, and then suddenly the peace is lost because of something small! Our faith is easily shaken! Every effort to get back there seems useless; meditating and praying do little to restore the peace we had tasted. If only we understand that it's because our own efforts won't get us there—only God can establish us in Jesus.

The same way justification isn't due to our own works, and we must just accept in faith the promise that God will give us life in Christ, so with sanctification, we need to stop striving to establish a stronger connection with Christ, and let God do it. *"God is faithful, by whom you were called into the fellowship of his Son, Jesus Christ our Lord"* (1 Cor 1:9). What we need is faith that being established in Christ is God's work—even though we are weak and unfaithful, He delights in doing it if we will trust Him.

Many can testify of the joy, contentment, and experience this faith brings. What peace knowing the vinedresser cares for the branch, making sure it grows stronger, and that its union with the Vine becomes more perfect, watching for danger, supplying everything it needs! What peace and rest to give our abiding into God's care, not worrying or praying it will happen, but realizing everything we do is because He is first doing the work in us!

Establishing us in Christ is His work: He does it by motivating us to watch, wait, and work. As long as we don't interrupt Him trying to do it ourselves—we just need to depend on Him in faith and open our hearts to let Him work. This frees us from care and responsibility! As our lives and the world rushes on; with all the temptations, worries, and trials that distract and lead to failure, how wonderful to be an established Christian—always abiding in Christ! How wonderful to have the faith that such a life is within our reach!

It is within your reach. It's God that establishes you in Christ. Understand that believing this promise won't just give you comfort, but is the key to achieving it. The Bible teaches us that faith was the one condition for God to show His power among His people. Faith is the stopping from all our own efforts, and depending on other things, Faith is being helpless, believing God's promise, and claiming its fulfillment. Faith is quietly putting ourselves in God's hands for Him to do His work. We need to let this truth become real to us: It's God Almighty, the Faithful and Gracious One, who will establish me in Jesus.

Look at what the Bible says about strengthening and establishing:

- "*The Lord will establish you as a people holy to himself*" (Deut 28:9).
- "*O Lord...direct their hearts toward you*" (1 Chron 29:18).
- "*God loved Israel and would establish them forever*" (2 Chron 9:8).
- "*You will strengthen their heart*" (Psalm 10:17).
- "*Now to him who is able to strengthen you*" (Rom 16:25).
- "*He may establish your hearts blameless in holiness*" (1 Thess 3:13).
- "*The Lord is faithful. He will establish you and guard you against the evil one*" (2 Thess 3:3).
- "*The God of all grace, who has called you to his eternal

glory in Christ, will himself restore, confirm, strengthen, and establish you" (1 Pet 5:10).

However up and down your spiritual life has been, however bad your character or situation is, these verses show that even you can be established by Him. You can become an established Christian. It's simple if you'll listen: As I am in Christ, then day by day I will be established in Him.

It's so simple, yet takes us so long to learn. The main reason is that God's grace for us is too big for us to comprehend; we don't take it for what it is. Once we see and accept what it brings, a wonderful change happens in our spiritual lives. Before, we just took care of ourselves, but now God takes charge of it. We are in God's school, He is a Teacher that plans with infinite wisdom what each of His pupils will learn, and delights when we come for our daily lessons.

We just need to stay in God's hands, and follow His guidance, not lagging behind nor going ahead. When we remember that it's God who works both to will and to do, we will surrender to His working. We won't worry about our hearts and their growth because the Father is the vinedresser who wisely cares that each plant is well secured. We will know the prospect of a life of strength and fruitfulness is real for all who take God as their hope.

A life of trust like this has to be a blessed one. Maybe there are times when you agree to this way of living and give your heart to your Father to care for. But somehow it doesn't last. You forget to give all the needs and cares of your spiritual life to the Father's charge, you feel anxious, burdened, and helpless. Isn't it because you haven't committed the job of remembering to surrender every day to Him? Memory is one of the greatest gifts we have: It links days and years together to keep a record of our life, and to know we are still ourselves.

In spiritual life, memory is also important. God has made a way even for the sanctifying of our memory. The Holy Spirit is the One that remembers, the Spirit of recollection. Jesus said, "*He will teach you all things and bring to your remembrance all that I have said to you*" (John 14:26). "*God who establishes us with you in Christ, and has anointed us, and who has also put his seal on us and given us his Spirit in our hearts as a guarantee*" (2 Cor 1:21-22). It's for establishing us that the Holy Spirit has been given. God's promises, and your faith and surrender to accept them—He will help you to remember these each day. The Holy Spirit is the memory of the Christian.

Add this to the promise that it is God who establishes us in Jesus. As you leave the worries of your growth and progress to God who establishes you in the Vine and feel the joy of knowing that He is in charge, ask and trust the Holy Spirit to remind you every day of your relationship with God. He will do it. Each morning your faith will grow stronger: God will see that each day I become more united to Jesus.

"*The God of all grace, who has called you to his eternal glory in Christ, will himself restore, confirm, strengthen, and establish you*" What more do you want or need? Expect it confidently, ask for it enthusiastically. Count on God to do His work. And learn in faith to sing the song, each new experience a note that becomes deeper and sweeter: "*Now to him who is able to keep you from stumbling and to present you blameless before the presence of his glory with great joy, to the only God, our Savior, through Jesus Christ our Lord, be glory, majesty, dominion, and authority, before all time and now and forever. Amen"* (Jude 1:24-25).

Yes, glory to God, who will establish us in Christ!

STUDY GUIDE

As much as we can read this book to understand and follow through these questions to help us, there is nothing quite so important as praying. Don't forget to take time out to spend with God, asking Him to show you more, asking Him to help you abide in Him. It's only by His power that we can enter and stay there. Even before tackling these study questions, go before Him.

1. What does being established in Christ mean to you?
2. Psalm 62 speaks of not being shaken. Would you say this sums up your Christian life or not? Why?
3. Murray quotes a few verses on God establishing Israel. What implications does this have for us?
4. It seems like a paradox that even when your Christian life is up or down, or your situation, you can still be established. Explain what you think this means.
5. Why is remembering so important in the context of being established? What is the Holy Spirit's role in this?
6. Go through 1 Peter 5:10. Look at the verbs used to

describe what God does for us. In your own words, explain each of them: *"restore, confirm, strengthen, and establish."*

7. Compare this with what it says God does for us in Jude 1.

13

EVERY MOMENT

"In that day, A pleasant vineyard, sing of it! I, the Lord, am its keeper; every moment I water it. Lest anyone punish it, I keep it night and day."
–Isaiah 27:2-3

The vineyard was a symbol of Israel, with the True Vine standing in the middle. The branch is the Christian, who lives in the Vine. The song of the vineyard is also the song of the Vine and all its branches. Those that watch over the vineyard are still called to bring every weak Christian in to be able to say, "*Sing of it!* **I, the Lord**, *am its keeper; every moment* **I water it**. *Lest anyone punish it,* **I keep it** *night and day."*

Is it possible for us to always abide in Jesus? Is a life of continuous fellowship with the Son of God possible while we live on earth? No! Not, if the abiding is our job, done in our strength. But things that are impossible with men are possible with God. If He keeps our hearts night and day, watches and waters them every moment, then the relationship with Jesus is possible to those who trust God to do what He says. Then the branch abiding in the vine day and night, summer and winter, in an unending fellowship, is the simple, certain promise of our abiding in Jesus.

No Christian can indeed abide in Jesus without interruptions; life happens. "*If anyone does not abide in me he is thrown away*" (John 15:6). But when the Savior says, "Abide in me," and promises that "*whoever abides in me and I in him, he it is that bears much fruit*" (John 15:5), He is talking about a willing, conscious, and whole-hearted surrender to accept this offer, and agree to abide in Him as the only life we choose. But can we voluntarily and consciously abide in Jesus without faltering? There are two reasons that we can't.

Our human nature is the one reason. We can't be occupied with two things at the same moment. We face hours every day at work where all our attention is on the tasks we have to do. How can we be mindful of Jesus, keeping fellowship with Him, while our concentration is on our work? Abiding in Jesus demands such effort and meditation on Him, that we'd have to remove ourselves from work and everyday life just to get it right. This is why the first monks isolated themselves.

But there is no need to remove ourselves from the world. Abiding in Jesus is not something that needs our minds and feelings to be totally concentrated only on Him every moment. It's committing ourselves to the Everlasting Love, having faith that He is always with us, watching and guarding us against evil, even when we are completely focused on other things. Our hearts have rest, peace, and joy knowing we are kept even when we can't keep ourselves.

There are many examples of love motivating and keeping our hearts, while our minds are focused on our work. A father has to leave home to work to supply the needs of his family. He loves his wife and children and longs to be with them. He spends hours without a moment to think of them, and yet his love is deep and real, motivating him with a secret joy in his work. A king has many duties, pleasures, and trials, but he does so as royalty, even when he is not thinking of it. A loving wife and mother never loses who she is to her husband and children: The awareness and the love are there, even in her busy, daily chores.

So, is it impossible for the Everlasting Love to keep our spirits, that we never lose awareness that we are in Christ, kept in Him by His almighty power? It is possible. We can be sure of it. Abiding in Jesus is more than a fellowship of love—it's a fellowship of life. Working or resting, the awareness of life never leaves us. The mighty power of Eternal Life in us maintains the consciousness of its presence. Jesus, who is our life, lives in us, making us aware that we are in Him.

The second reason we can't be continually aware is sin. Sinning every day is something we see as inevitable. It's just something that happens, and so we can't continually abide in Jesus—we will be unfaithful and fail. But because of this sinful nature, abiding in Him was given so that we would be delivered from it! The Heavenly Vine has almighty power to keep us close! He would never say "abide in me" without giving us the grace and power to do it! The vinedresser will keep us from falling, as He promises: "*Every moment...night and day!*"

When we see God as the Keeper of Israel, who "*will keep you from all evil; he will keep your life*" (Psalm 121:7), we will learn to believe that conscious abiding in Christ every moment, night, and day, is what God has prepared for us.

Let this be your aim. I know it's not easy to achieve; there will be times of struggle and failure. If the church was what it should be—where older Christians are examples of God's faithfulness to younger Christians, like Caleb and Joshua, encouraging the people to go and possess the land by saying, "*Let us go up at once and occupy it, for we are well able to overcome it*" (Num 13:30). If the churches' atmosphere is a healthy, trustful, joyful consecration, then abiding in Christ would grow naturally in Christians.

But the state that many churches are in—sick and weak—anyone who desires to abide in Jesus will be put off by the depressing life around them. This should warn and urge us to give ourselves more to Him. If you feel like giving up, be encouraged—only believe. He who has put the blessing within your reach will lead to take hold of it.

The way our hearts find it may be different. For some it may come as the gift of a moment: In times of revival, in fellowship with other Christians that the Spirit is working in, being led by a servant of God who can guide, and sometimes in solitude. It's as if a new revelation suddenly comes to the heart. It can see the strong Vine holding and bearing the weak branches that there is no more doubt. How it ever understood the words to mean something else, is a mystery. To abide unceasingly in Christ is for every believer. The heart can now see it. Believing, rejoicing, and loving happen naturally as a result.

For others, it's a slower and more difficult path. Day by day, the soul has to press forward through disappointment and hardship. Be encouraged, this will also lead to rest. Hold on to the promise that the Lord says, "*I keep it night and day.*" Hold on to those words: "*Every moment.*" There you'll find His love and your hope. Be content with nothing less.

Don't think anymore that life's duties, worries, and sins will stop you from the abiding life of fellowship. Rather, let your mouth speak a language of faith: "*For I am sure that neither death nor life, nor angels nor rulers, nor things present nor things to come, nor powers, nor height nor depth, nor anything else in all creation, will be able to separate us from the love of God in Christ Jesus our Lord*" (Rom 8:38-39). In this, He is teaching me to abide.

If things look dark and your faith is failing, sing again the song of the vineyard: "*I, the Lord, am its keeper; every moment I water it. Lest anyone punish it, I keep it night and day.*" And be confident that, if Jehovah keeps the branch night and day, and waters it every moment, a life of continuous fellowship with Christ is most definitely our privilege.

STUDY GUIDE

Murray moves onto very practical ground in this and the next few chapters. For us, as normal people, living 24 hours a day, working, and raising families, often our spiritual lives take a backseat. But he still believes it is possible for us to maintain this solid relationship in Jesus despite all the distractions and demands of life. Be open about what you face, talk about it, write it down, bring it to the Lord. This is how we reflect on where we are, and how we can grow.

1. What does it mean, that what is impossible for us is possible for God? Look at Luke 18:27 for the context of this verse.
2. What is the first reason that we can't abide in Jesus without faltering? Do you face this issue sometimes in your own life?
3. Have you ever felt you needed to hit pause or remove yourself from the world to get it right? Why is this not necessary?
4. What is the second reason for not being able to abide without losing our way?
5. Which one of the two reasons is the greater obstacle for you in trying to abide in Jesus?
6. How does the state of the church encourage or discourage the thought of a daily relationship with Jesus? Which one does your church belong to?
7. Read over Romans 8:38-39 again. Take time to go over every single instance listed and see these for your own life and how God's love is greater than all these things

14

DAY BY DAY

"And the people shall go out and gather a day's portion every day."
–Exodus. 16:4

One portion for each day: This was the rule for God's giving and man's working regarding the manna in the desert. It's the same law for God's grace and His children. Understanding the beauty and application of this arrangement will help us, who are weak, to have confidence and perseverance to hold on throughout our lives. A patient who was in a bad accident asked the doctor: "How long do I have to lie here?" The doctor's answer: "Only a day at a time." This taught the patient a precious lesson. It was the same for God's people: *"A day's portion every day."*

Because of man's weakness, God graciously appointed day and night. If we had been given one long, unbroken day, it would have exhausted and overwhelmed us. The change of day and night is there to restore our strength. Just as a child is only given the lesson for the day which it can cope with instead of the whole book, so it is with us, if there were no divisions in time.

Broken down and divided into parts, we can bear them. We only have to worry about and do the work for that day. The night is a time to refresh and give us a fresh start for each new morning. The mistakes of the past can be left behind and learned from. We only have to be faithful for one short day; the long years and a long life take care of themselves, without ever needing to be a burden.

What an encouragement the life of grace is to us. But many people get depressed thinking about gathering and keeping the manna they need to travel through the desert for so long. They haven't learned the comfort of those words: "*A day's portion every day.*" That takes away all worries about tomorrow. Today is yours; tomorrow is the Father's.

Do you know if you will still abide in Jesus after all the years of cold, temptation, or trials? You shouldn't have to worry about that. Manna, as your food and strength, is given only for each day. It is faithful to fill you in the present and is your only security for the future. Accept, enjoy, and fulfill the part you have to perform today. His presence and grace today will remove all doubt of whether you can trust Him for tomorrow.

This lesson is a very valuable one! We get sidetracked at looking at the bigger picture of life and neglect the smaller snapshot of today. We forget that it's the single days that make up the whole, and the value of each day depends on its influence on the whole. A lost day is a broken link in the chain, which often takes extra days to fix. A lost day has a chain reaction, making it more difficult to keep on track the next one. One lost day might even cost you what months or years of hard work had built up. Many Christians will agree with stories of their own.

If you want to abide in Jesus, let it be day by day. We've already spoken about moment by moment, but the lesson of day by day has something more to teach. There are many moments that don't require focus and thought from you; abiding is in the depths of the heart, kept by the Father, to whom you entrusted yourself. But this is something that needs to be renewed each day—renewal of surrender and trust to live moment by moment.

God has gathered up the moments into a bundle, that we might consider them. As we look forward in the morning, or look back in the evening, and weigh the moments, we learn how to value and use them properly. And as the Father meets you each morning with the promise of enough manna for the day, meet Him with the renewal of placing yourself in His beloved Son. Get used to this as one of the reasons God gave us day and night. He thought of our weakness and provided for it.

Let each day's value come from you agreeing to abide in Christ. As the sun rises, say: "One day only, given to abide and grow up in Jesus Christ." If it's a day of health or sickness, joy or sorrow, rest or work, struggle or victory, let your main thought be this: "A day that the Father gave; in it, I must become more closely united to Jesus."

The Father asks, "Can you trust me just for this one day to keep you abiding in Jesus, and Jesus to keep you fruitful?" You can joyfully respond: "I will trust and not be afraid."

Each day's portion was given to Israel very early in the morning. It was for use and nourishment during the whole day, but giving and getting the portion was the morning's work. If you want to spend the day properly and abide all day in Jesus, it depends on the morning hour. If the firstfruits are holy, the lump is holy (Rom 11:16). The first offering determines the whole outcome.

During the day, there are busy hours of work and dealing with people, and only the Father can maintain our connection with Jesus. The morning manna lasted the whole day. Only when we take time on our own to renew our fellowship with Jesus can abiding be kept up all day. In the fresh, quiet of the morning, we can look at the day ahead. With Jesus, we can think through our duties and the temptations that may come and give it all to Him who will be everything to us. Christ is our manna, our nourishment, our strength, our life. We can take the day's portion—Christ—and go on knowing that the day will be one of blessing and growth.

And as the lesson of the value and work of the day is understood, we will find the secret of "*day by day regularly*" (Ex. 29:38). Each day of faithfulness brings a blessing for the next. Trust and surrender become easier and more wonderful. And so the Christian life grows: As we give our whole heart to the work of each day, it becomes all the day, and then every day. Each day on its own, the whole day regularly, day by day as they come, we abide in Jesus. These days make up our lives: What was once too huge to achieve is now ours when we are content to take and use "*the daily burnt offerings by number according to the rule, as each day required*" (Ezra 3:4).

Even now we will be able to hear Him say: "*Well done, good and faithful servant. You have been faithful over a little; I will set you over much. Enter into the joy of your master*" (Matt 25:23). Our life becomes a wonderful exchange of God's daily grace and our daily praise: "*Blessed be the Lord, who daily bears us up*" (Ps 68:19); "*as I perform my vows day after day*" (Ps 61:8).

We learn to understand God's reason for daily giving, as He gives us enough for each day. And we ask and expect only enough for the day. We begin to number our days not from sunrise, or by our work, or the food we eat, but the daily renewal of manna—the joy of daily fellowship with Him, the Life, and the Light of the world. Heavenly life is as continuous as our earthly one. Abiding in Christ each day has its blessing for that day. We abide in Him every day, the whole day. Lord, make this our portion.

STUDY GUIDE

This chapter is wrapped up in the image of God providing manna for His people in the desert every day—just enough. If you have time, it would be good to recap that story and gain insight into it within its context. Reading Exodus 16 will be enough to give you the broader picture. As you read it again, substitute the idea of manna and water for whatever it is that you depend on the Lord for every day, in your time, life, and space. This will help greatly to understand it more for where you are right now.

1. What is the purpose of God creating day and night?
2. Are you an "in-the-moment" person or a long-term planner that is constantly thinking of tomorrow? Does this affect your reliance on God sometimes?
3. Look at Matthew 6:34 and James 4:13. What do you understand about these? Do they apply to what Murray is talking about?
4. What is the consequence of one lost day? What is meant by 'lost' in this context?
5. What is the significance for us of gathering manna in the morning?
6. In terms of this chapter, what is our manna? How do we gather and get it?
7. Now, looking at Matthew 6:11, what is your understanding of what Jesus was teaching His disciples in this prayer?

15

AT THIS MOMENT

*"Behold, **now** is the favorable time; behold, **now** is the day of salvation."*
−2 Corinthians 6:2

Living moment-by-moment is so important when abiding in Christ. The way to learn it is to practice living in the present moment. When you have time to think of Jesus—if you're praying, or in passing—say to yourself: "Right now, I abide in Jesus." Don't waste those moments on feeling sorry about when you haven't abided fully, or won't be able to abide, just stand on the promise: "I am in Christ; this is the place God has given me. I accept it and rest in it. I now abide in Jesus."

This is how we learn to abide continually. You might feel weak, shy, or unworthy to say, "I am abiding in Jesus;" but every moment, as the weakest person agrees to take their place as a branch in the Vine, can say, "Yes, I abide in Christ." It's not about feeling, or growth or strength, it's simply about whether we agree to take our place in your Lord at that moment. If you're a believer, you're in Christ. If you're in Christ and want to stay there, then at that moment, say, "Blessed Savior, I abide in You now. You keep me now." One of the deepest secrets of faith is in those words.

At the end of a conference on spiritual life, a prominent minister said that he didn't know that he'd learned anything new, but he'd learned how to use what he already knew. He'd learned that it was his privilege at each moment, whatever was happening around him, to say, "Jesus saves me now." This is the secret of rest and victory. If I can say, "At this moment, Jesus is life, strength, and peace," I only have to rest and realize it's what I need just for that moment. Seeing I am in Christ, my faith is strengthened and my heart is at peace: Now I abide in Christ.

When we are striving to find how to abide in Christ moment to moment, remember that the door is: Abide in Him at this present moment. Instead of wasting our efforts trying to get into a state that will last, just remember that it is Jesus who keeps us. Have faith in Him for the present moment: This is the only way to be kept until the next moment.

A life of permanent and perfect abiding hardly ever happens all at once: It comes mostly step by step. So, grab every opportunity of trusting in the present moment. When you pray, start with the words: "Father, I am in Christ; I now abide in Him." When things are busy and you have a moment to think, say: "I am still in Christ, abiding in Him now." Even when you have sinned and your heart is unsettled: "Father, I have sinned; but I still come in Christ. There is no other place I can be; I now abide in Christ." In every circumstance, every moment of the day, He calls you to abide in Him now. Even as you're reading this, enter the life of always abiding by doing it right now.

David wrote a beautiful passage that can help make this clearer (2 Sam. 3:17-18). He had been anointed king in Judah. The other tribes still followed Ish-bosheth, Saul's son. Abner, Saul's chief captain, decided to rather lead the tribes of Israel to submit to David, the God-appointed king of the whole nation. He speaks to the elders of Israel: *"For some time past you have been seeking David as king over you. Now then bring it about, for the Lord has promised David, saying, 'By the hand of my servant David I will save my people Israel from the hand of the Philistines, and from the hand of all their enemies'."* And they followed and anointed David to be king over all Israel, as well as Judah (2 Sam. 5:3). We can learn a lot from this about the way a person is led to a life of surrender and undivided allegiance to full abiding.

First, there's the divided kingdom: Judah faithful to the king God chose; Israel clinging to the king they chose. The nation was divided and had no power to conquer its enemies. It's a picture of the divided heart. We accept Jesus as King; but the surrounding territory, the everyday life, is not under His rule; half is ruled by our self-will. There is no real peace within and no power over our enemies.

But there is a desire for a better kingdom: *"For some time past you have been seeking David as king over you."* When David conquered the Philistines, Israel had believed in him; but they were led astray. Abner appeals to their own knowledge of God's will, that David must rule over all. So as Christians, when we first came to Jesus, we wanted Him to be Lord over all, our only King. But doubt and self-will came in, and we didn't allow Jesus to have power over our whole life. And yet we are not content. We long for something better.

God's promise comes through. Abner says: "*The Lord has promised David, saying, 'By the hand of my servant David I will save my people Israel from the hand of the Philistines, and from the hand of all their enemies'.*" David had conquered the Philistines, so only he could conquer their enemies now.

It's the same as our hearts are invited to trust Jesus for the victory over every enemy, and a life of complete fellowship. "*The Lord has promised*"—this is our only hope. "*As he spoke by the mouth of his holy prophets from of old, that we should be saved from our enemies and from the hand of all who hate us; to show the mercy promised to our fathers and to remember his holy covenant, the oath that he swore to our father Abraham, to grant us that we, being delivered from the hand of our enemies, might serve him without fear, in holiness and righteousness before him all our days*" (Luke 1:70-75). David reigning over every corner of the land and leading a united and obedient people to victory: This is the promise of what Jesus can do for us when we surrender our whole life to Him to be kept abiding in Him.

Abner said that they had been wanting David as their king for a while, and then added, "*Now then bring it about.*" Do it now is the message of this story if we desire to give Jesus complete control. Whatever the present moment is, even if we are unprepared, however, divided and hopeless our lives may be, surrender—this very moment.

It will take some time as He brings your life into order—conquering enemies and training you for His service. It doesn't all happen instantly, but some things can and do. The one thing is you surrendering yourself entirely to live only in Him. As time goes on, and your faith has become stronger, this surrender will be more real and understood. But it can't wait. The only way to start is to begin at once. Do it now. Surrender yourself this very moment to always abide in Jesus. It's the work of a moment.

Christ's renewed acceptance of you is also the work of a moment. He has you and holds you as His own, and that every time you say, "Jesus, I abide in You," there is an immediate response. No act of faith is in vain. He takes hold of us and draws us close to Himself. So, every time we hear or think of abiding in Him, do it at once. Listen to the whisper: Do it now.

The blessing of the present moment is passed on to the next. It's the unchanging Jesus that links them together, and the power of living continually in Him that takes hold of you. It may seem to be a small thing, but as you do it in this moment, it is the beginning of the ever-present now, which is the mystery and the glory of eternity. So, abide in Christ: Do it now.

STUDY GUIDE

Murray continues with his practical direction of bringing the topic of abiding into our everyday lives. It will be a very good exercise to look at your daily and weekly timetable and see where your time is being spent. If you don't have one, it can be good to draw one. Be honest—if there is very little time for the Lord, don't be condemned. This is where we learn and grow, by exposing areas that we need to look at and possibly change.

1. Murray talks about wasting our efforts "trying to get into a state that will last." Has this happened to you? What do you feel about this?
2. According to the chapter, how does a life of permanent and continuous abiding come about?
3. Look again at the story from 2 Samuel. Right now, where do you see yourself—under David or Ish-bosheth?
4. What two things stop us from allowing Jesus to reign completely over our lives? Are these present in your life now?
5. Do it now. At this moment. Do you struggle with this type of command? Why?
6. What is it that we need to do right now in order to enter into an abiding relationship?

16

FORSAKING ALL FOR CHRIST

"I have suffered the loss of all things and count them as rubbish, in order that I may gain Christ and be found in him."
–Philippians 3:8-9

Wherever there is life, there is a continual exchange of taking and giving, receiving, and restoring. The food I take is given out again in the work I do; the impressions I receive are expressed in my thoughts and feelings. The one depends on the other—giving out increases the power of taking in. The enjoyment of life is found in giving and taking.

It's the same in spiritual life. Some Christians only see the joy in receiving; they don't know that the ability to receive is only through continual giving. It's only in the emptiness of letting go of what we have, that the divine fulness can flow in. Jesus often mentioned this. When He spoke about selling everything to secure the treasure, of losing our life to find it, of the abundance to those who forsake all, He was explaining self-sacrifice as the law of the Kingdom for Himself as well for His disciples. For us to abide in Christ, and be found in Him, we must be able to say as Paul did, "*I count everything as loss because of the surpassing worth of knowing Christ Jesus my Lord...and be found in him*" (Phil 3:8-9).

What is there to forsake or give up? First, there is sin. You can't be properly born again without giving up sin. But often, the young convert doesn't fully understand what sin really is, what God's holiness is, and the power of Jesus to conquer sin, so giving up sin is only partially done. As the Christian grows, so does a deeper desire to get rid of everything unholy. When the desire to abide in Christ, and be found in Him, becomes strong, then we see how much more we need to surrender. We see that we need to die to sin in Christ and everything that is sin.

In the Spirit, we surrender to sin no more—to only be servants of righteousness. We do it gladly, knowing that every sin surrendered is a benefit for us—it makes room for the infilling of the presence and love of Christ.

Giving up everything unrighteous, we then need to give up everything self-righteous. This goes against everything we have achieved or are good at, and it takes a long time for us to really understand what it means to not allow self in any service of God. Unconsciously, we let our minds, hearts, and will have free reign in God's presence. In prayer and worship, in Bible reading and working for God, instead of depending only on the Holy Spirit's leading, we think we can do what we can't. We are slow to learn the lesson, *"for I know that nothing good dwells in me"* (Rom 7:18).

As we learn this, we see how corrupt we really are, we see that we can't abide in Christ without giving up all that is of self—without giving it up to death, and waiting for the Holy Spirit to work in us what is acceptable in God's sight.

What about our whole natural life? We were created by the Creator, with all our gifts, talents, and skills. When we're born again, we want to serve Him with everything we have. It's a good desire, but that alone is not enough. So much harm has been done in the church because Christians think that using their gifts is naturally what they must do.

A special grace is needed here, and the only way it can come is through sacrifice and surrender. Even though I am born again, I must see that all my gifts and skills are still corrupted by sin, and under the power of the flesh. I can't use them for God's glory. I must first lay them at Jesus' feet, to be accepted and cleansed by Him. I must realize that I can't use them properly on my own. They are dangerous to me, because through them the flesh, the old nature, self, will use its power.

Realizing this, I must give them up to the Lord. When He has accepted them and set His stamp on them, I receive them back as His property, to wait on Him for the grace to use them properly under His influence. The path of entire consecration is the path of full salvation. What is given up is received back again to become our own, but also forsaking all is followed by receiving all. We abide in Christ more as we forsake all and follow Him. As I count all things rubbish for His sake, I am found <u>in</u> Him.

The same principle applies to what we do and what we have. It was the same with the fishing nets on the Sea of Galilee and the household duties of Martha. Jesus taught them to forsake all for Him. It was not some casual command, but applying a law in nature to the Kingdom of His grace—if the old occupant is properly thrown out, the new one can properly take ownership, and the renewal of everything within can be complete.

This principle goes even deeper. The spiritual gifts of the Holy Spirit within us, surely these don't need to be given up and surrendered? They do! The exchange of giving up and taking in is a life process, and must not stop. As soon as we receive something, it begins to grow old and become stagnant. It's only into an empty heart that the streams of living waters flow. The secret to never being thirsty is always thirsting for more.

Each experience we receive as a gift of God must be returned to Him immediately, in praise and love, in self-sacrifice and service. Then it can be restored to us again, fresh and beautiful with the fragrance of heaven. This is the lesson we learn from Isaac on Moriah. Wasn't he the son of promise, the God-given life (Rom.4:17)? And yet he had to be given up, and sacrificed, that he might be received back again more precious than before—an example of the only begotten Son of the Father, whose pure and holy life had to be given up before He could receive it again in resurrection power, and bring us into it. It's also an example of what takes place in the Christian. Instead of becoming content with wonderful things that have happened, we press on, forgetting and giving up all that is behind and reaching out to take hold of Jesus.

Is surrendering everything to Him a single step, the act, and experience of a moment, or is it something that has to be done daily as a progressive achievement? It's both. There may be a moment in your life when you have a revelation of this truth, and in one act, lay yourself on the altar as a living and acceptable sacrifice. These moments are sometimes the change between being lost and a failure to abide and live in His power. Even then, you don't stop, but through prayer ask how you can surrender more, offering up all you have to God.

If you will abide in Christ, then this is the path. Our human nature is scared of self-denial and crucifixion when it comes to our own lives. But what we hate doing and can't do, grace will do, and give you a life of joy and glory. Just surrender yourself to Jesus; the conquering power of His presence will give you joy as throw out everything you thought was precious to you.

Mark Chapter 10 verse 30 uses the phrase, "*A hundredfold now in this time.*" These words of Jesus come true to all who accept His commands to forsake all. Receiving soon makes giving up more wonderful. The secret of abiding can be seen in this: As I give myself completely to Christ, I find the power to take Him completely for myself; and as I lose myself and all I have for Him, He takes me completely for Himself, and gives Himself completely to me.

STUDY GUIDE

Well done on making it this far! The halfway mark in a month-long transformation of our minds and our hearts. There is so much that has been discussed already, and if you are normal, you are probably already forgetting, or afraid you will forget, most of it! Keep that notebook going! Get into the habit of writing down your answers. Discuss with others to broaden your own thinking on the subject.

1. The giving in this chapter is not the same as distributing goods and finances. What giving is Murray talking about?
2. We need to give up the unrighteous and the self-righteous. Which one is harder for you?
3. What, according to Murray, has brought the church some of the most harm?
4. There is even that we need to give up. What are these other things? Why do you think these may surprise many or be overlooked?
5. Explain this paradox: "The secret to never being thirsty is always thirsting for more."
6. Matthew 19:16-22 is a passage we may have heard often and not totally understood. In the light of this chapter, what do you see?
7. Why is our human nature scared of self-denial and crucifixion?

17

THROUGH THE HOLY SPIRIT

"But the anointing that you received from him abides in you...just as it has taught you, abide in him."
−1 John 2:27

What a beautiful thought; to always abide in Christ! The more we think about it, the more attractive it seems. And yet many new Christians just sigh when they hear the call, "Abide in me," They understand so little what it really means, and don't realize how it can be achieved. They just need someone who can make it clear, and remind them that it is possible. If they would just listen to this verse, they would have such hope and joy! These words tell us that the Holy Spirit will teach us everything, especially how to abide in Christ.

But there's always someone who isn't encouraged by this verse, it only depresses them more. It speaks about something else that they don't know how to get right: How to understand when the Spirit is teaching, or how to hear His voice. If they don't know the Teacher, then the promise of His teaching about the abiding doesn't help much.

This kind of thinking is a common mistake among Christians. They imagine that the Spirit has to reveal spiritual mysteries that they have to try and understand and then act on. God doesn't work like this. Spiritual truth works the same as abiding in Christ: We must live and experience truth in order to know it. Living with Jesus is the only school for the science of heavenly things.

"What I am doing you do not understand now, but afterward you will understand" (John 13:7). This is a law of God's Kingdom. Receive what you don't comprehend, submit to what you can't understand, accept and expect what seems to be a mystery, believe what looks impossible, walk in a way which you don't know—these are the first lessons in the school of God.

"If you abide in my word, you are truly my disciples, and you will know the truth" (John 8:31-32). These words show there is a habit of mind and life that goes before understanding. True discipleship is following first and then knowing the Lord. The believing surrender to Christ, and the submission to His word to expect what appears most improbable, is the only way to the joy of knowing Him.

These principles are the same for the way the Spirit teaches. He guides us to what God has prepared for us, without us knowing how. On God's promise, and trusting in His faithfulness, we surrender to the leading of the Holy Spirit, without trying to understand in our minds what He is going to do, but letting Him do His work. Afterward, we will find out what He has done there. Faith trusts the Spirit to work in the deep areas of our hearts without us being able to see any of it.

So, the word of Christ and the gift of the Spirit are guarantees that the Spirit will teach us to abide in Christ. By faith, we rejoice in what we don't see or feel: We know, and are confident that the Spirit is working, guiding us into abiding and having a full relationship with God. The Holy Spirit is the Spirit of life in Jesus; it's His work, not only to breathe, but to strengthen, and perfect the new life inside us. And as much as we surrender to the unseen Spirit of life working within us, our faith will become knowledge. The Spirit will reveal in the Bible what has already been done in our lives by His power.

Apply this to the promise of the Spirit teaching us to abide in Christ. The Holy Spirit is the mighty power of God. He comes to us from the heart of Jesus, the revealer and communicator of Jesus in us. When we say, "the fellowship of the Spirit," we are taught what His work is. He is the bond of fellowship between the Father and the Son: By Him, they are one. He is the bond of fellowship between all Christians: By Him, we are one. Above all, He is the bond of fellowship between Christ and Christians. He is the sap through which Vine and the branch grow in union: By Him, we are one.

We can be certain that if we believe in His presence and working, and are careful not to grieve Him as He is in us, and wait and pray to be filled with Him, He will teach us how to abide. First, He will guide our will into submission to Jesus, then build up our faith, then breathe peace and joy into our hearts, and teach us to abide. Then from our hearts and lives, He will bring understanding so that we will know the truth—not just ideas of truth, but the truth in Jesus, the light of what He has already made a reality in our lives. *"The life was the light of men"* (John 1:4).

Now, it should be clear that if we want the Spirit to guide us into the abiding life, we first need quiet faith. With all the questions and difficulties we may have as we strive to abide in Christ; with all the desire to have an experienced Christian help us along; with the awareness of failure, ignorance, and helplessness, we must hold on to this: We have the Holy One to teach us to abide in Him.

*"But **the anointing** that you received from him **abides in you**... just as it has taught you, **abide in him**."* These verses about abiding should become our practice of faith. As you are in Jesus, you have His Spirit too. Believe He will do His work with power, as long as you don't stop Him. Believe He is working, even when you can't see it. Believe He will work if you ask the Father for it. It's impossible to live a life of abiding without being full of the Holy Spirit. Believe the fulness of the Spirit is your daily portion.

Spend time in prayer before the throne of God and the Lamb, from which the river of the water of life flows. Only there can you be filled with the Spirit. Make this a daily habit, honoring Him by the quiet confidence that He is doing His work within. Let your faith make you jealous of whatever could grieve Him—the spirit of the world or anything of self and the flesh. Let your faith grow in the Bible and all it says of the Spirit, His power, His comfort, and His work. Let your faith in the Spirit inside you, lead you to look to Jesus.

The anointing we received from Him, only grows stronger when we are focused on Him—Jesus is the Anointed One. As we look to Him, the holy anointing comes, *"It is like the precious oil on the head, running down on the beard, on the beard of Aaron, running down on the collar of his robes!"* (Psalm 133:2). Faith in Jesus brings the anointing; the anointing leads to Jesus, and to abide in Him alone.

Abide in Christ, in the power of the Spirit. Is abiding still a fear or a burden? Definitely not. If we really knew how gracious our Holy Comforter is, and how wonderful it is to surrender to His leading, we would experience the comfort of having such a teacher to bring us to abide in Christ. The Holy Spirit was given for this one purpose—that the redemption and life in Jesus would be made known to us. We have the Holy Spirit to make Jesus' saving power and victory over sin present within us. This is what makes Him the Comforter: We don't have to mourn an absent Christ.

So, as we read, meditate, and pray about abiding in Christ, consider it settled that the Spirit of God is in us, teaching, guiding, and working. Let's rejoice in the confidence that we will succeed in our desire to live in Jesus because the Holy Spirit is working with secret, divine power in the heart that doesn't block Him by unbelief.

STUDY GUIDE

As with everything else in Christianity, to know about it is not the same as knowing it. There is a deeper element where we must trust and allow the Holy Spirit to bring it to our hearts as a revelation, and not just sit in our minds as knowledge. These study questions can guide you only so far, but the rest will have to be through an open heart, a bowed knee, and a willing surrender for Him to teach.

1. What is your understanding of how the Holy Spirit teaches us?
2. What is the law of the Kingdom that Murray is talking about in this chapter? Why is it hard for us to accept?
3. In the analogy of the vine and branches, what role does the Holy Spirit take?
4. What is the first thing we need if we want the Holy Spirit to teach us to abide in Christ? Why do you think this comes first?
5. Is it possible to abide in Jesus without having the Holy Spirit?
6. What is the purpose of the Holy Spirit for us?
7. Why is He called the Comforter?

18

IN STILLNESS OF SOUL

"In returning and rest shall ye be saved; in quietness and confidence shall be your strength."
–Isaiah 30:15

"Be still before the Lord and wait patiently for him."
–Psalm 37:7

"For God alone my soul waits in silence."
–Psalm 62:1

The Christian life is sometimes viewed as a partnership, where God and man each have to do their part. In this alliance, man doesn't have much to do, and whatever he brings is sinful anyway, but he must still do his utmost. Only then will God do His part. If you share this view, then the verses that speak of us being still and doing nothing, resting and waiting to see God's salvation, become difficult to tie in.

When we speak of quietness and not striving as the secret, you will see it as a contradiction.

However, this is what the Bible teaches. When God and man are spoken of as working together, there is no partnership where each must contribute their share of the work. The relationship is very different. The actual idea is cooperation through dependence. Just as Jesus depended on the Father for all His words and works, so the Christian can do nothing of himself. What he can do of himself is sinful.

So, he must stop and wait for God to work in him. As he stops all his own efforts, faith takes over to show that God does what He has promised, and works in him. What God does is renew, sanctify, and awaken his heart. The amount he surrenders as a tool for God to use will be the amount God uses him as an instrument of His power. When we realize the combination of perfect passivity with the highest activity, we will have the deepest experience of the Christian life.

A quiet heart—the stillness of soul—is one of the most important and beneficial lessons we can learn in abiding in Jesus. God reveals His ways to those who are meek and patient. This type of spirit can be seen in the three Marys:

- The one who answered, "*Behold, I am the servant of the Lord; let it be to me according to your word*" (Luke 1:38), when she was visited by the angel; and even with all that happened around her, it was said, "*Mary treasured up all these things, pondering them in her heart*" (Luke 2:19).
- The one who "*sat at the Lord's feet and listened to his

teaching" (Luke 10:39), and when she anointed Him for His burial, showed a much deeper understanding of His death than even the disciples.
- The one who looked for Jesus in the Pharisee's house, and could only speak with her tears (Luke 7:38).

A quiet heart before God is the best preparation for knowing Jesus, and for holding on to the blessings He gives. When the heart is in silent awe and worships before God, the still, small voice of the Spirit will be heard.

As you try to understand how to abide in Jesus, think on this: "*For God alone, O my soul, wait in silence, for my hope is from him*" (Psalm 62:5). Do you want this union with the Heavenly Vine? People can't reveal it to you, only the Father. You have to admit your own ignorance and inability; the Father will give you the teaching of the Holy Spirit. If you listen, bring your thoughts under control, and prepare your heart to wait on God to hear what He has to say, He will reveal His secrets to you.

One of the first secrets, as you become nothing before Him, quiet and listening to His still voice, is that He will teach you what you could not hear with all the noise of your efforts and thoughts. You will learn that all you have to do is listen, hear, and believe what He promises; to watch, wait, and see what He does; and in faith, worship, and obedience, surrender to His working.

This should be one of the most amazing things we hear, that all we have to do is rest and be quiet so that God will work for us and in us. But it's not always like that! We are so slow to learn that being quiet is contentment, strength, and our greatest work—the secret of abiding in Christ! Let's try to learn it and watch out for the many things that threaten and interfere with this.

We waste our time as we allow our hearts to become filled with things of this world. We must be diligent in our work and lives and do these to our best abilities, but even in these, we must be careful. We must discern what we do and don't get involved in. If abiding in Jesus is our first priority, then we must not get easily distracted. Even in our daily duties and tasks, we can become so occupied that there is little time for fellowship with God. We are quickly filled with worry and anxiety about these things that eat away at our trusting Him—we are tossed back and forth on a troubled sea. We can't hear the gentle whispers of the Holy Comforter there.

Fear and suspicion of spiritual things will have the same effect. All the worry and striving don't allow us to hear what God has to say. There is only unrest when we try our own way and in our own strength to find spiritual blessings. When our hearts are occupied with our own plans and efforts to do God's will and find a way to abide in Jesus, we will always fail. Our interference blocks God's work. He can only do His work only when we stop our attempts. He will do His work in the heart that honors Him by expecting Him to work.

Sometimes, when our hearts are desperate to enter into a life of faith, we become impatient, and then condemn and judge by our human standards of where we think we should be.

That is why we need to be still, and accept His word: "*In quietness and in trust shall be your strength*" (Isaiah 30:15). If we want to hear the Father, we will pause and wait until our hearts are quiet before we just read the Bible. Knowing how quickly self can intrude and assert itself in the holiest moments, we must surrender our hearts in a quiet act of surrender to the teaching and working of the Spirit. Then we will be still and wait in holy silence until we are calm and ready to receive His revelation and presence. Our reading and prayer will become waiting on God with our ears and heart open to receive what He says.

"Abide in Christ!" Don't think you can do this if you don't have a daily quiet time, meditate, and wait on God. As you go out into the world with its distractions, train your heart to find the peace of God that passes all understanding, to keep your heart and mind. Only in a quiet, calm heart, the life of faith can take root, the Holy Spirit can teach, the Father can do His work. Every day, we must learn to say, "*For God alone my soul waits in silence.*"

When we feel it is too difficult to get this right, we only have to look and trust in Him—He can calm the storm. Encourage quiet in your life as a way to abide in Christ; expect the quiet and calm of heaven as the fruit of abiding in Him.

STUDY GUIDE

The reason Murray termed this book a 31-devotional, is not just because we are devoting every day to making sure we read through a chapter, but also because we are devoting time to God for Him to teach and guide us. The best, and often the only way, is to do this in quiet and solitude. If you have been reading through this book as a group, that's still fine, but make sure that "quiet time" is also part of it for your personal reflection and revelation.

1. What is your view of the partnership spoken of at the beginning of this chapter? Is it something you share or shared?
2. How is dependence different from a partnership? What does it entail?
3. Do you find it easy to be quiet before God? Why or why not? What do you think should change?
4. What is meant by the "noise of your efforts and thoughts?"
5. Murray lists quite a few things that can block, interfere, and deafen us. List them and see which ones you struggle with the most.
6. The life of faith can only take root in what? Why is this so?
7. We know the verse that says, "Be still and know I am God." But reading it in context might open our understanding a bit more. look at Psalm 46 as a whole. What do you see?

19

IN SUFFERING AND HARDSHIP

"Every branch that does bear fruit he prunes, that it may bear more fruit."
–John 15:2

There isn't a plant like the vine that suits the image of our relationship to God. Its fruit and juice are so full of spirit, so stimulating, but it also has a tendency toward evil—to turn into wood that's only good for the fire. More than others, it's a plant that needs to be pruned often and always, and depends heavily on proper training and cultivation. The harvest is one of the most rewarding for the vinedresser.

In His parable, Jesus refers to the need to prune the vine, and the blessing it brings. He shares a picture of hope to our suffering and sorrow, comfort to the bleeding branch in its time of hardship: "*Every branch that does bear fruit he prunes, that it may bear more fruit.*" When trials come, and we're shaken in our confidence, moved from our place of abiding in Christ, His voice comes loudly, calling us to abide even closer. Especially in tough times, abide in Christ.

Abide in Christ! This is the Father's plan in sending hardships. In the storm, the tree digs its roots deeper in the soil; in the hurricane, the people are grateful to be able to stay inside the shelter of the house. In suffering, the Father wants to lead us more deeply into the love of Christ. Our hearts wander from Him when wealth and pleasure tempt us away. We are so easily satisfied by these things, and our relationship with Jesus takes a back seat.

It's the Father's mercy to bring discipline, to make everything dark and unattractive so that we feel our sin even more and find no joy in what was leading us astray. He does it so that when we find our rest in Jesus in times of trouble, we learn to choose to abide in Him as our only option. When the trial is over and we've grown more firmly into Him, even in prosperity, He will be our only true joy. He is so committed to this, that despite the pain He allows, He will not hold back to guide His children to come home and abide in the Son. In every trial, pray for the grace to see the Father pointing back to Jesus, and saying, abide in Him.

Abide in Christ: Then you will enjoy all the blessings God has for you in the suffering. God's wisdom in this will become clear to you. Your confidence in His love will become stronger, and His Spirit will bring about the promise: "*He disciplines us for our good, that we may share his holiness*" (Heb 12:10).

Abide in Christ: The cross you have to carry is to have fellowship with His cross. It will also reveal its secrets—the curse He took for you, the death to sin you have with Him, the love he brings as a High Priest into all your sorrows.

Abide in Christ: Through His sufferings, you will have a deeper experience of His love.

Abide in Christ: In the furnace, the Son of Man will come, removing all the impurities to refine you like gold, so that Jesus' will be reflected in you.

Abide in Christ: Your strong flesh will be shamed, your impatience and self-will humbled, to make place for the humility of Christ. As Christians, we can go through these trials but gain very little from them. Abiding in Christ is the secret to gaining everything the Father wants to bring us through His discipline.

Abide in Christ: In Him, you will be comforted. Comfort comes before benefit in hardships. Even though the Father's main aim is for us to improve and grow through the trial, He doesn't forget to comfort us. When He does, it's to turn the bleeding heart to Himself, for us to have fellowship with Him. When He doesn't, His aim is still the same.

Bringing us to holiness is where we find comfort. The Holy Spirit is the Comforter, because He makes us holy, and brings us into a close relationship with Jesus. He teaches us to abide in Christ; and because God is found there, the truest comfort will be there too. In Jesus, the heart of the Father is revealed, for us to rest in His arms. In Him, love is revealed, as tender and compassionate as a mother. In Him, we are given way more than what we have lost—He takes from us, that we might have more room for Him. In Him, suffering is made holy, a taste of eternal glory. Would you want to have comfort in hardship? Abide in Christ.

Abide in Christ: Then you will bear much fruit. No vine is planted without the owner thinking of the fruit it will bring. Other trees may be planted for their beauty, shade, or wood—the vine is only for fruit. The vinedresser constantly looks to see how it can bring more fruit.

Abide in Christ in times of suffering, and you will bear more fruit. The deeper experience of Christ's tenderness and the Father's love will urge you to live to His glory. The surrender of self and self-will in suffering will prepare you to sympathize with the misery of others. The softening that comes through discipline will make you ready to be the servant of all, just like Jesus. The Father's desire for fruit through pruning will bring you to surrender yourself again and to have but one aim—making known and showing His wonderful love to others.

You will learn to forget self. In suffering, you will begin to pray more for others. When you see hardship coming, accept it in Jesus. When it comes, feel that you are in Jesus more than in the trial, for He is closer to you than any suffering. When it's finished, carry on abiding in Him. Just think of Jesus as He speaks of pruning, and the Father's desire as He does the pruning: *"Every branch that does bear fruit he prunes, that it may bear more fruit."*

Your times of hardship will become times of blessing—preparation for fruitfulness. Times when you are led into closer fellowship with the Son of God, and deeper experience of His love and grace. Times when you are established in confidence that He and you belong to each other—more satisfied with Him and given to Him than before, Times when your will is crucified, and your heart is brought into deeper harmony with God's will. Times when you will be a pure vessel for the Master's use, prepared for every good work.

Christian, try and learn the truth, that in suffering your calling is to abide in Christ. Spend time with Him; beware of the comfort and distractions that friends bring. Let Jesus be your companion and comforter. Delight yourself in knowing that a closer relationship with Him, and more abundant fruit, are the results of any trial because it's the vinedresser who is pruning. He will bring the desire of your heart as it surrenders to His work.

STUDY GUIDE

Being honest and vulnerable in answering and discussing is one of the quickest ways to grow. In doing so, you will clearly see areas that need attention or weaknesses that require more help from the Lord. It's easy on your own, but harder in a group. But with others, you will find that by confessing those things, you are now accountable to keep them before Jesus until he has changed you. Otherwise, we can so easily sweep them under the carpet after we've admitted things to ourselves.

If it's a respected person in the church or someone who can walk with you through this time, take the step and confide in them. They cannot change you, but Jesus can, and with a heart that is willing to be open, He will!

1. When you hear the word suffering and hardship, does it go against what you picture as the Christian life?
2. What is your response to reading a phrase like the "Father's plan in sending hardships?"
3. Do you think there is a connection between our suffering and the 'discipline' spoken of in Hebrews?
4. What do surrendering and discipline prepare us for?
5. What is the aim of all the suffering and the hardship, according to this chapter? How does this happen?
6. How does this relate to James 1:2-4?
7. Is there a difference between suffering that God allows and suffering that we bring on ourselves through our own actions?

THAT YOU MAY BEAR MUCH FRUIT

"Whoever abides in me and I in him, he it is that bears much fruit,"
–John 15:5

"By this my Father is glorified, that you bear much fruit,"
–John 15:8

We all know that fruit is the product of the branch for us to eat. It's not for the branch, but for us to take from the branch. As soon as the fruit is ripe, the branch drops it off, to begin bearing fruit again for another season. A fruit tree doesn't live for itself, but for those who are refreshed and nourished by its fruit. So, the branch exists only for the sake of the fruit. Its only aim then is to make the vinedresser happy—that's its safety and glory.

This is a beautiful picture of us as Christians abiding in Christ! We don't just grow stronger in our relationship with the Vine, but we bear fruit. We can offer it to others so they can eat and live. To everyone around us, we become trees of life that refresh others. We are a blessing to all we know and meet, because we abide in Christ, and receive the Spirit and the life to give to others. If you want to be a blessing, abide in Christ; if you abide, you will definitely bless others. The same way the branch that abides in a fruitful vine bears fruit, so, too, will the person that abides in Christ with His blessing be made a blessing.

It's easy to see that if Jesus, the heavenly Vine, has taken the Christian as a branch, then He has promised to supply the sap, spirit, and nourishment to help it bear fruit. "*From me comes your fruit*" (Hosea 14:8). These words give new meaning to our parable. Your heart only has one worry—to abide closely and completely. He will give the fruit. He will do everything to make the Christian a blessing.

Abiding in Him, you receive His love and compassion towards sinners, giving you a desire to see them saved and helped. Our hearts are naturally selfish. Even as Christians, we are only concerned with our own salvation and happiness. But abiding in Jesus, we find His never-ending love. Its fire begins to burn in our hearts. We see the beauty of love and want to love, serve, and save others because it's the greatest privilege we can have.

Abiding in Christ, our hearts learn to feel how lost the sinner is, and their disregard for God. With Jesus, we begin to bear the burden of souls, the burden of other people's sins. As we become closer to Him, the passion that motivated Him to the cross is found in us, and we are ready to follow His footsteps, to put aside our own happiness, and devote our lives to win the people that Jesus has taught us to love. The spirit of the Vine is love. That spirit of love flows into the branch that abides in Him.

The desire to be a blessing is only the start. Soon we are aware of our own weakness and how difficult it is. People are not born again despite what we say. We want to give up, pull back. But as we abide in Christ, we receive new courage and strength to carry on. Believing what Jesus says, that He will give His blessing to the world through us, we see that we are only instruments through which Jesus' power works. His strength is perfected in our weakness.

Admitting we are weak, but carrying on, convinced the Lord is working through us, is a huge step forward. We can rejoice that the strength to do it is from God, not us. Remembering that we are united with Jesus, we don't even think about our weakness, but trust in power. This confidence changes the way we look, brings a gentle firmness to our speech, and perseverance to all our efforts, which all play a part in influencing the lost. We carry on in the spirit of victory; for this is the victory that overcomes, even our faith. It's not humility when we say God can't bless our unworthy efforts. We claim and expect a blessing because it's Jesus that works in us.

The great secret of abiding in Jesus is a deep conviction that we are nothing and He is everything. When we learn this, then our weakness is no longer an obstacle to His saving power. If we surrender to Jesus to do His work in simple, childlike trust, we will bear much fruit. We won't be afraid of our part in the promise: "*Whoever believes in me will also do the works that I do; and greater works than these will he do, because I am going to the Father"* (John 14:12). We expect to have a blessing, not thinking we have to be unfruitful in order to be humble. The branches heavy with fruit bow down the lowest. Abiding in Christ, we have surrendered to the agreement between the Vine and the branches: The fruit is for the glory of the vinedresser.

Let's learn two lessons: The first is that if we are abiding in Jesus, we must begin to work. Let's have the heart to influence those around us. Let's accept our calling, that we are servants of the love of Jesus to others. Our aim every day must be to make an impact for Jesus. When you look at the branch, you see its resemblance to the Vine. We must live so the holiness and gentleness of Jesus shine out in us. We must live to represent Him.

Life must prepare the way for teaching. The church and the world need men and women that are full of the Holy Spirit and love, and as instruments of the grace and power of Jesus are witnesses for Him, and for His power on behalf of all Christians. If we long to see people born again, let us offer ourselves to Him to work through. There is work in our homes, among the sick, poor, and the homeless. There is work in a hundred different paths that the Spirit opens through us if we will be led by Him. There may be work perhaps in ways that haven't been opened by others yet.

Abiding in Christ, let's work. Not like those following the trends and doing their minimal religious duties. Let's work as those who are growing more like Christ because they are abiding in Him, and count winning souls as a joy and glory of heaven here on earth.

The second lesson is if you work, abide in Christ. One of the blessings of work, if it's done in the right spirit, it will deepen your relationship with Jesus. Your weakness will be exposed and throw you back on His strength. It will cause you to pray more; and as you pray for others, your heart unconsciously grows deeper in Jesus. The true nature of branch's dependence is that it gains everything from Him and is independent of all else because it's dependent only on Jesus.

If you work, abide in Christ. There are temptations and dangers. Sometimes people get drawn away by the work they're doing for Jesus, and it's taken the place of fellowship with Him. Work sometimes gives a form of godliness without the power. As you work, abide in Christ. Let a living faith in Jesus working in you be the source of all your work. This will inspire humility and courage. Let the Holy Spirit live in you as His compassion and power.

Abide in Christ and offer yourself completely to Him, to keep your body holy for His use. For Jesus to work through us, we need to consecrate ourselves to Him every day. This is abiding in Him and should be our greatest privilege and happiness. To be a branch bearing much fruit—nothing less, nothing more—should be our only joy.

STUDY GUIDE

Reading the entire passage of John 15 again will help. Often, we read portions of the Bible and see one thing, but when we read it again, a new thing leaps out at us. This is the Holy Spirit making the Word of God alive to us. It can just be words, or it can be a spiritual guide, a love letter, or a necessary encouragement when our hearts are open to being shown what He intends us to learn and hear.

Take the time to read. Take the time to listen and hear. Take the time to accept.

1. What is the aim and purpose of a fruit tree? What is our aim as a branch abiding in Christ?
2. What is the purpose of bearing fruit?
3. Look at Galatians 5:22-23. Do you see any of these in your own life? Which ones are missing?
4. What do you understand about the thinking of not bearing fruit in order to be humble? Why does Murray say this is a mistake?
5. Doesn't the first lesson we must learn go against everything Murray has already taught about relying on, resting, and letting God do the work?
6. What is the second lesson and how does it tie in with the first one?
7. What are the dangers of this work that is being spoken of?

21

SO YOU WILL HAVE POWER IN PRAYER

"If you abide in me, and my words abide in you, ask whatever you wish, and it will be done for you."
–John 15:7

Prayer is one of the ways to find, and one of the fruits of a relationship with, Christ. As a way, it's incredibly important. All the things of faith, the pleadings of desire, the longings to surrender more, the confessions of failure and sin, the denying of self and clinging to Jesus, are found in our words of prayer.

Often when we learn something new, our first instinct is to look to the Father and ask for understanding of what we have just seen in the Bible. But the Christian who is not content with this spontaneous impulse and takes time in prayer to wait and take hold of the revelation will really grow strong in Christ. Either way, our prayer will be heard, and we will find that prayer is one of the great ways of abiding more abundantly.

But it is not as a way, but as a fruit, that Jesus speaks of prayer in the parable of the Vine. Here, it is not a way for us to get blessings for ourselves, but as one of the channels for all the benefits of salvation to be distributed to the world. The glory of the Father and the extension of His Kingdom are the reason we have been made branches. If we abide in Him, we will have power with God and man. Like Elijah, our prayer will be the effective, intense prayer that achieves much. This prayer will be the fruit of our abiding in Him and the means of bearing much fruit.

For the Christian not abiding completely in Jesus, the difficulties with prayer can steal the comfort and strength it's supposed to bring. How can someone so unworthy expect to have influence with God? This is the wrong idea of humility. Compared to God's sovereignty, His wisdom, and love, this Christian can't see how any prayer can make a difference. They pray, but it's more because they must than from faith that the prayer will be heard.

But to those who truly abide, there are no such questions and confusion. They realize that they are heard and accepted in the spiritual unity they share with Jesus. A relationship with Jesus is for life: We are one with Him, our prayer goes up to the Father as if it's His prayer. Because we abide in Him, we can ask what we will, and it's given to us.

There are many reasons for this. One is that by abiding in Christ, and having His words in us, we learn to pray according to the will of God. Our own will is kept down, our natural thoughts and wishes are taken captive by the thoughts and wishes of Jesus. We have the mind of Christ—everything we do comes into harmony with His. We continually check if our surrender is complete, praying that nothing may be kept back. Everything is surrendered to His life in us, that it may sanctify even our wishes and desires. The Holy Spirit breathes through our whole being, and without knowing it, our desires conform with God's will and are fulfilled. Abiding in Christ renews and sanctifies the will: We ask what we will, and it is given to us.

Abiding in Jesus teaches us in prayer to only seek God's glory. Jesus' one thought in answering prayer (see John 14:13) is this, "*that the Father may be glorified in the Son.*" In His intercession on earth (John 17), this was His one desire. In heaven, it is the same. As we abide in Christ, He breathes this desire into us. Only the glory of God becomes the priority of life in Jesus.

At first, we become quiet, not wanting anything, afraid that it's not to the Father's glory. But once we accept and surrender everything to it, we lift up, enlarge, and open our hearts to the glory of God. Abiding in Christ, we don't just learn to desire, but to spiritually discern what will be for God's glory. An acceptable prayer is when, as the fruit of its union with Jesus, the whole mind is in harmony with He said: "*Father, glorify your name*" (John 12:28).

Abiding in Christ, we can confidently call on the name of Jesus. Asking in someone's name means we are authorized by the one who sent me to ask as if he himself is asking. Christians often try to think of the name of Jesus and try to convince themselves to have faith that they will be heard, while they feel they have no real faith in His name. They are not living in Jesus' name.

It's only when they pray that they want to use the name. This is not right. The promise, "*Whatever you ask in my name*" (John 14:13), can't be separated from, "*Whatever you do, in word or deed, do everything in the name of the Lord Jesus*" (Col 3:17). If the name of Jesus is at my disposal, so that I may use it for all I will, it must be because I am at His disposal, so that He has free and full command of me. Abiding in Christ gives the right and power to use His name with confidence.

To Jesus, the Father refuses nothing. Abiding in Christ, I come to the Father as one with Him. His righteousness and Holy Spirit are in me. The Father sees the Son in me and gives me what I ask. Some think that through credit or imputation, the Father sees us as if we were in Christ, even though we're not in Him. No, the Father wants to see us living in Him. Then our prayer will really have power. Abiding in Jesus doesn't just bring us to pray correctly but gives our prayers His power.

Abiding in Christ also increases faith that receives an answer. "*According to your faith be it done to you*" (Matt 929). This is one of the laws of the kingdom. "*Believe that you have received it, and it will be yours*" (Mark 11:24). This faith is more than "God promised, I receive." Faith depends on the words being alive in us. Without fasting and prayer (Mark 9:29), without humility and a spiritual mind (John 5:44), without total obedience (1 John 3:22), there can't be living faith.

But when we abide in Jesus and grow in our relationship with Him, where He does everything and makes my prayers acceptable, we can expect an answer because we are one with Him. By faith, we learned to abide in Him. The fruit of that faith grows to a larger faith in all that God has promised to be and do. We learn to say prayers in quiet confidence: We know we have what we ask of Him.

Abiding in Christ also keeps us in the place where the answer can be given. Some Christians pray for blessings, but when God comes to bless them, they can't be found. They never thought the blessing must not only be asked, but waited for, and received in prayer. Abiding in Christ is the place for receiving answers. An answer not received in God would be dangerous—we would use it on our selfish desires (Jas. 4:3). Many answers—for spiritual grace, or for power to work and bless—can only come when we experience who Jesus is to us. Everything is in Him. Abiding in Him is what brings power to prayer because the answer is in Him.

Abide in Christ, for this is the school of prayer—mighty, effective, answered prayer. Abide in Him, and you will learn what so many can't understand: The secret of the prayer of faith is the life of faith—the life that abides in Jesus.

STUDY GUIDE

As you read and spend time going through this book, pray. It is one of the keys to a deep spiritual life. It's also one of the ways we ask for understanding about what we've just read and for receiving knowledge from God. We can often rush through the text and hope the Lord will show us something, but as we've already seen, only by being still before Him, will we find answers and grow.

How to Pray Effectively by R. A. Torrey is a good, solid book that can open your eyes to how, when, and why we as Christians pray.

1. How can prayer be a fruit? Are there more fruits than the nine spoken of in Galatians 5?
2. Asking what we will, and God giving it to us—do you agree with this or not?
3. What is the difference between praying in Jesus' name and living in Jesus' name?
4. This faith is more than "God promised, I receive." What does this mean?
5. What does it mean to have power in prayer? Have you ever experienced this before?
6. "Some Christians pray for blessings, but when God comes to bless them, they can't be found." What do you understand about this?
7. If you had to rate your prayer life (1-not effective at all, to 10-very effective), what would you give yourself?

22

AND IN CHRIST'S LOVE

"As the Father has loved me, so have I loved you. Abide in my love."
–John 15:9 [1]

Lord, open our eyes to see what this verse tells us about Your love, that we may enter and stay there. How else can we learn about such love?

Before Jesus invites us to abide in His love, He first tells us what that love is. This emphasizes His invitation so that it's impossible not to accept: *"As the Father has loved me, so have I loved you!"*

"As the Father has loved me." Love is who He is. It's not a characteristic, but His very nature that all His characteristics come from. Because He is love, He is the Father, and there is a Son. Love needs to be given away and be united to someone. Because God is love, there must be a Father and a Son. The love of the Father to the Son is the reason He delights in

the Son, and says, "*This is my beloved Son with whom I am well pleased*" (Matt 3:17).

Divine love is like a burning fire. It's intense and infinite with one aim and joy: The only-begotten Son. Looking at all God's characteristics—His infinity, perfection, immensity, majesty, omnipotence—seeing them like the rays of His love, we still don't get a proper picture of His love. Even though it's beyond our understanding, it's still a picture of how Jesus loves us.

As His redeemed, He delights in us and longs for us, with a love that is stronger than death, and many waters cannot quench. His heart desires for us, seeking our fellowship and love. He would die for us again if it was necessary. As the Father loved the Son, and could not live without Him—so Jesus loves us. His life is linked to ours. We are more precious to Him than we will ever know. We are one with Him. "A*s the Father has loved me, so have I loved you.*" What love!

It's an eternal love. Before the world was made, Christ was to be the head of His church, a body that would demonstrate His glory. He loved and longed for those the Father had given Him in eternity. When He came and told His disciples that He loved them, it was not with a love of earth and time, but with an eternal love. It's this same love that calls us to abide in Him. "*I have loved you with an everlasting love*" (Jer 31:3).

It's a perfect love. It gives everything, holding nothing back. "*The Father loves the Son and has given all things into his hand*" (John 3:35). Jesus loves you the same way—all He has is yours. He sacrificed His throne and crown for you: He thought nothing of giving His blood for you. His righteousness, Spirit, glory, and throne, are all yours. This love holds nothing back to make you one with itself in a way we can't imagine. What incredible love, to love us just as the Father loved Him, and to offer us this love.

It's a gentle, tender love. When we think of the Father's love for the Son, we see how worthy of that love the Son was. When we think of Christ's love to us, there is nothing but unworthy sin. How can that holy, perfect love be the same as the love for sinners? Can it be the same? It is. The nature of love doesn't change, even if what is being loved is different. Jesus only knows this love that His Father loved Him with.

Our sin only emphasizes the beauty of love even more, even in heaven. With tender compassion, He meets us in our weakness, with incredible patience He puts up with us, with the gentle kindness He meets our fears and failures. It's the love of the Father to the Son made beautiful as it is brought to our level for us.

And it's an unchangeable love. "*Having loved his own who were in the world, he loved them to the end*" (John 13:1). "*For the mountains may depart and the hills be removed, but my steadfast love shall not depart from you*" (Isa 54:10). It begins with this promise: "*For I will not leave you until I have done what I have promised you*" (Gen 28:15). Our evil hearts were the reason love first came. Our sin that often brings nothing but grief, fear, and doubt is the reason it still holds and keeps us. Why? For no other reason than this: "A*s the Father has loved me, so have I loved you.*"

The motive, measure, and means of surrendering ourselves to abide in Him are found in this love.

Love gives us a motive. You just have to look and see how it stands, pleads, and prays. See the pleading gentleness of the crucified love as it stretches out its pierced hands and says, "Won't you abide with me? Won't you come and abide in me?" It points us to heaven, to the cross, and all it has done as proof of how much it wants to win us over. It reminds us of all it has promised to do if we run into its arms. It asks if we're satisfied with how it has treated us since we responded to its call.

With such authority and tenderness that we could mistake it for a rebuke, it says, "A*s the Father has loved me, so have I loved you. Abide in my love.*" There can only be one answer to such pleading: Jesus, here I am. Your love shall be the only home of my heart: In Your love, I will abide.

Love is also the measure of our surrender to abide in it. Love gives everything but also asks everything in return. It doesn't do it out of a grudge, but because it's the only way it can take hold of us and fill us. It was the same in the Father and Son's love; it is the same in Jesus' love to us, and must be the same when we come to abide in His love. Our surrender to love must be the same measure it surrenders to us.

If we only knew the blessings and joy for us in love, and that what we give up will be rewarded even greater in this life! If we understood its height, depth, length, and breadth that goes beyond human knowledge! Then we wouldn't even think it's a sacrifice or surrender, but be filled with wonder at the privilege of being loved with such a love, of being able to abide in it forever.

Is it possible to always abide in His love? If this question pops up, just see how love is made as the only way to abide in Him: Faith in that love enables us to abide in it. If this love is so intense and passionate, then you can definitely depend on it to keep you. If that's true, then all your weak and shameful ways won't be able to block it. If this love is so powerful, then you can trust that it's stronger than your weakness. Its mighty arms will hold you tight and never let you go.

There is only one thing God asks of us. Having given us the power of free will to choose, He cannot force this on us but waits until we willingly give Him access to our hearts. The sign of this agreement is faith. Faith for our wicked sin be saved in the arms of love, and our weakness to be made strong. The love that the Father loved the Son! The love that the Son loves us! I can and do trust it to keep me abiding in Jesus.

Note

[1] It's difficult to understand why one Greek word in John 15 should have three different translations in the English Bible: The original word abide is *abide* in verse 4, *continue* in verse 9, and *remain* in verses 11 and 16.

STUDY GUIDE

The Love of God: An Intimate Look at the Father-Heart of God by Oswald Chambers is just one of many books that will really open your eyes to see God's love. Another is *Love of God* by Charles Spurgeon, although this is more a sermon than an entire book. To get to grips with what God's love is will take us right into heaven! There is no end to it. But getting a glimpse, and understanding it enough to take hold of us, will change our lives.

Spend time asking Him to show you His love. It's one of the things He enjoys doing and will answer that prayer in incredible ways.

1. What do you understand about God's love for you?
2. What do you understand about the statement that love is not a characteristic of God?
3. Love is the motive, measure, and means for us to surrender to God. What do you understand about this?
4. Does your sin, weakness, or unworthiness block you from His love? Why or why not?
5. Look at 1 John 4:16. How does this equate with what we have already looked at in terms of God and love?
6. What is the one thing God asks of us?
7. How does faith come into this equation?

23

AS CHRIST IN THE FATHER

"As the Father has loved me, so have I loved you. Abide in my love. If you keep my commandments, you will abide in my love, just as I have kept my Father's commandments and abide in his love."
–John 15:9-10

Jesus had already taught His disciples that abiding in Him was abiding in His love. His time of suffering was coming near, and there wasn't more to be said. They must have had many questions about abiding in Him and His love. He knew this, and let His own life speak as an example. They would have to look at Jesus abiding in the Father's love, and this relationship would make their union with Him clear. His life in the Father was the law for their life in Him.

Understanding this incredible concept might be difficult, but it's such a clear example that we must take notice of it. We find it in the verse, *"As the living Father sent me, and I live because of the Father, so whoever feeds on me, he also will live because of me*" (John 6:57). And when Jesus prays "*that they may be one even as we are one, I in them and you in me*" (John 17:22-23). The relationship of Christ with the Father and His life in Him is all our thoughts and expectations should be fixed on to live and abide in Him.

The first time we hear of Jesus' life in the Father, we see that they were one—one in life and one in love. This was the root of Him abiding in the Father. While Jesus was on earth, He knew He was one with the Father; that the Father's life was in Him, and His love on Him. Without this knowledge, abiding in the Father and His love would have been impossible. So, this is the only way that we can abide in Christ and His love. Know that you are one with Him—one in the unity of nature. By being born a human, Jesus took on your nature to be one with you. When you are born again, you become one with Him and share in His divine nature. This link is as real and close as the one that linked Him to the Father—the link of a divine life. You have as much right to Jesus as He has to the Father. Your relationship with Him is just as close.

Because it's the union of a divine life, it's also one of infinite love. Enduring humiliation on earth, He had the joy strength of knowing He was the recipient of an infinite love, and of living in it every day. He wants you to learn the secret of rest and joy from His example. You are one with Him: Surrender yourself to be loved by Him; open your eyes and heart to the love that shines and fills you. Abide in His love.

Also, think of the method of abiding in the Father and His love as the law of your life. "*I have kept my Father's command-*

ments and abide in his love." Jesus' life was submission and dependence, and yet it was blessed. The thought of dependence and submission makes our proud minds think only of humiliation and serving. But to Jesus, they are the secret of joy and contentment.

The Son is not afraid to lose everything by giving it all up to the Father, for He knows that the Father loves Him, and is only focused on His beloved Son. He knows as much as He depends on the Father, is the amount the Father will give of Himself. So, when He said, *"The Son can do nothing of his own accord, but only what he sees the Father doing,"* He carries on to say, *"For whatever the Father does, that the Son does likewise. For the Father loves the Son and shows him all that he himself is doing"* (John 5:19-20).

The Christian who studies Jesus' life as the example and the promise will understand that the verse, *"Apart from me you can do nothing"* (John 15:5), is the beginning for, *"I can do all things through him who strengthens me"* (Phil 4:13). He learns to boast in weakness and take pleasure in trials and suffering for Jesus' sake; because *"when I am weak, then I am strong"* (2 Cor 12:10). He rises above the way many Christians speak of and live in their weakness because he's learned from Jesus that emptying himself and sacrificing his will is the only way to have this life of love with everything in it. Dependence, submission, and self-sacrifice are as much for the Christian as they were for Jesus. As He lived through and in the Father, so we live through and in Christ.

Glory and honor as a Christian must be seen in the Father's love. Jesus gave Himself completely to the Father's will and glory, and the Father crowned Him with glory and honor. He recognized Him as His only representative. He allowed Him to share in His power and authority. He exalted Him to share His throne as God. It is the same for us if we abide in Jesus' love.

If we give ourselves and our interests to His love, deny our desire for our own will and honor, completely depend on Him in all things, content to have no life except in Him, He will do for us what the Father did for Him. He will honor us: As Jesus is glorified in us, we are glorified in Him (2 Thess. 1:12). He recognizes us as His worthy representatives; He trusts us with His power; He hears our prayers, to influence the way He manages the church and the world; He gives us His authority and influence over men. His Spirit only lives in this kind of heart as instruments for His work. This is the life of love for us if we abide in Jesus' love, even as He is in the Father's!

Abide in the love of Christ. Take His relationship to the Father as a guarantee of what your own can become: Blessed, mighty, and glorious. You won't see abiding as a burden and a work and be afraid of it. The example of Jesus' life in the Father will be an incredible rest in your relationship with Him, an overflowing fountain of joy and strength. To abide in His love, His mighty, saving, keeping, satisfying love will be yours, just as He was in the Father's love.

Because our calling is so great, it's not something we can achieve through work, or we have to perform. As it was with Jesus, it should be the result of the spontaneous life flowing from inside us, and the work of God's love.

The only thing we need to do is take time and study the example Jesus set for us. We need to be still before God, looking at Jesus' life in the Father until it becomes clear, and His voice whispers to us the same teaching He gave to the disciples. Be still and listen. Make every thought quiet until it has entered your heart: "Child! I love you, even as the Father loved me. Abide in my love, as I abide in the Father's love. Thy life on earth in me will be the perfect reflection of mine in the Father."

Isn't it impossible, can it be true? Just remember, the size of the privilege is justified by the size of His love for those He calls. Christ was the revelation of the Father on earth. He couldn't be that if their unity was not perfect—the complete communication of all the Father had to the Son. But He could be because the Father loved Him, and He stayed in that love. Christians are the revelation of Christ on earth. They can't be unless there is perfect unity, so the world can know that He loves and has sent them. But they can be if Christ loves them with the infinite love that gives itself and all it has and if they abide in that love.

Lord, show us Your love. Help us to know the love that's beyond our understanding. Lord, help us to see in Your own life what it means to abide in Your love. When we see this, it will be impossible for us to want any other life than the life of abiding in Your love.

STUDY GUIDE

Understanding the relationship of the Father and the Son is not easy to digest in one chapter. As with anything to do with God, it's often accepting the fact before we fully comprehend it. There is also an added obstacle of seeing God through the lens of our own earthly fathers, which tends to skew things slightly. We need faith, the Holy Spirit, and time to let God sift this incredible union down into our hearts.

The Fatherhood of God by Charles Spurgeon is a wonderful book continuing his sermon on this topic. Another excellent book to enlighten you further is by A.W. Tozer, *The Attributes of God Volume 2: Deeper into the Father's Heart.*

1. In your own words, describe the relationship of the father and the Son.
2. A few times, Murray says that we need to study the example Jesus set for us. What is this example?
3. Why do you think Jesus was able to live completely for His Father's glory and not His own?
4. What were the benefits for Jesus denying Himself so that His Father may receive all the honor?
5. What are our benefits in denying ourselves for the same reasons?
6. Look at John 10:25-30. How does this relate to what we are learning about in this chapter?
7. What is your view of God the Father? Is it anything like what Jesus saw of His Father?

24

OBEYING HIS COMMANDMENTS

"If you keep my commandments, you will abide in my love, just as I have kept my Father's commandments and abide in his love."
–John 15:10

This verse shows very clearly where good works fit in a Christian's life. Jesus as the beloved Son was in the Father's love. He kept His commandments, and so He stayed in the love. So, the Christian, without any works of his own, receives Christ and is in Him. He keeps the commandments and abides in the love.

When a sinner who wants to come to Jesus tries to do it by his own effort and works, the Bible warns that it is *"not a result of works."* Now that he is in Jesus, his flesh will come and try to persuade him that the Christian life is "not a result of works." But the Bible says clearly that we were "created in Christ Jesus for good works" (see Eph.2:9-10). To the sinner that's not born again, works and effort can be the biggest obstacle that keeps him from a relationship with the Savior. But to the believer that is in Christ, works are strength and blessing, for through them faith is made perfect (James 2:22), the relationship with Jesus is cemented, and the heart is more deeply rooted in the love of God. "*If anyone loves me, he will keep my word, and my Father will love him*" (John 14:23). "*If you keep my commandments, you will abide in my love.*"

The link between keeping the commandments and abiding in Jesus' love can easily be understood. Our relationship with Jesus is not something of the brain or emotions, but a real union in heart and life. The holy life of Jesus, His feelings and character, is breathed into us by the Holy Spirit. As Christians, we are called to think, feel, and want what Jesus thought, felt, and wanted. We don't just want His grace but also His holiness—holiness is the beauty of grace. To live the life of Jesus is to be delivered from our lives of self. Jesus' will is the only path from the slavery of our evil self-will to freedom.

For those that are too lazy to see, or too ignorant to try understanding, there remains a huge difference between the promises and commands of the Bible. The promises are a comfort and delight, the commands are not. But to those who really want to abide in Jesus' love, the commands are just as precious. They are the revelation of divine love, guides to a deeper experience of the divine life, helpers to a closer relationship with the Lord.

Having our will in harmony with His will is one of the main elements of our fellowship with Him. The will is as important in God as it is in humans. The will of God is the power that rules the moral and natural world. How can there be fellowship with Him without delighting in His will? As long as salvation is nothing but a personal safety for the sinner, then he will be careless or afraid of doing God's will. But when it's properly revealed through the Bible and the Holy Spirit—the restoration of our relationship and conformity to God—then there is nothing more natural or more beautiful than keeping Jesus' commandments. This is the way to abide in His love. It's a joy when the measure of the Spirit, and life of the Father and the Son in the Christian, depend on keeping His commandments (John 14:15,16,21,23).

Another thing that brings deeper understanding and acceptance of this is that Jesus didn't abide in the father's love any other way. On earth, His obedience was a reality. The evil power that caused man to rebel against God came to seduce Him too. As a human, the temptations to gratify his flesh were very real. To refuse them, He had to fast and pray. He suffered in temptation. He had to be clear about not wanting to do His own will, as a surrender He had to do this continually. Keeping the Father's commandments as the main aim of His life, He could abide in His love.

Doesn't He tell us, "*I do nothing on my own authority, but speak just as the Father taught me. And he who sent me is with me. He has not left me alone, for I always do the things that are pleasing to him*" (John 8:28-29). So, He showed us the way to a joyful life on earth in the love of heaven. When His Spirit flows in the branches, we are inspired to keep His commands as one of our greatest privileges.

If you want to abide in Jesus, keep His commandments. Keep them in the love of your heart. Don't keep them as a handy verse in the Bible, but through meditation, prayer, acceptance, and the Spirit's teaching, let them be written on your heart. Don't be content with just knowing the usual commands most Christians try to follow, ignoring the other ones. Under the New Covenant, there is more than agreeing with those of the Old Testament: "*I consider all your precepts to be right*" (Psalm 119:128). There is much of your Lord's will that you do not yet understand. Let Paul's prayer for the Colossians, "*that you may be filled with the knowledge of his will in all spiritual wisdom and understanding*" (Col 1:9); and of Epaphras, "*that you may stand mature and fully assured in all the will of God*" (Col 4:12), become your own.

One of the great elements of spiritual growth is a deeper knowledge of God's will for you. Don't think that consecration is the end of a holy life, it's only the beginning. Paul teaches us to lay ourselves on the altar, complete and holy offerings to God, but then goes further to tell us what that kind of life is: Always being "*transformed by the renewal of your mind, that by testing you may discern what is the will of God, what is good and acceptable and perfect*" (Rom 12:1-2). The progressive renewal of the Holy Spirit leads us to become like-minded with Christ. Then we receive spiritual perception—a holy instinct—where our "*delight shall be in the fear of the Lord*" (Isa 11:3).

We will know what and how to do the Lord's commands in our daily lives when ordinary Christians can't. If we keep them and hide them in our hearts, we will taste the blessings of someone whose "*delight is in the law of the Lord, and on his law he meditates day and night*" (Psalm 1:2). Love will absorb the commands into our hearts like food from heaven. They will no longer be a law that is apart from and against us, but a living power that brings our will into perfect harmony with all Jesus asks of us.

Obey. Haven't you promised to never tolerate sin anymore? "*I have sworn an oath and confirmed it, to keep your righteous rules*" (Psalm 119:106). Pray to be perfect and complete in God's will. Ask for any hidden sins to be revealed—anything not in perfect harmony with His will. Walk in the light faithfully, surrendering yourself to obey all that the Lord has spoken. When Israel took that vow (Exodus 19:8, 24:7), it wasn't long before they broke it again. But the New Covenant gives us the grace to make the vow and keep it too (Jer 31). Don't disobey, even in little things. Disobedience dulls the conscience, darkens the hearts, reduces our spiritual energies—so keep His commandments with complete obedience. Be a soldier that asks for nothing else but the commander's orders.

And if the commandments become heavy, just remember who they belong to. They are the commandments of Him who loves you. They are love, they come from His love, they lead to His love. Each time we surrender and sacrifice to keep them, we are led to a deeper relationship in the Savior's will, spirit, and love. We receive a double reward: A greater understanding of His love, and greater obedience to His life. These words will become a treasure: "*If you keep my commandments, you will abide in my love, just as I have kept my Father's commandments and abide in his love.*"

STUDY GUIDE

By now, if you have been following the readings and working through the questions, you should be cultivating a habit of studying God's Word. This is one of the reasons Murray set the book out into daily portions, rather than one book with a few lengthy chapters. By taking the commitment of a chapter a day, a healthy habit has been formed—spending time searching to understand God, His love for us, and how we can enter into that calling to abide even more.

1. What commandments are being spoken of in this chapter—the 10 commandments?
2. How do we keep commandments if it is not by effort or works?
3. What happens to us when we falter and don't keep some of His commandments?
4. How are Gods' will, commandments, and obedience connected?
5. According to Murray, what does disobedience do?
6. Look at 1 Samuel 15:22. What do you understand by this verse on obedience?
7. What must we do when the commandments become too heavy for us?

THAT YOUR JOY MAY BE FULL

"These things I have spoken to you, that my joy may be in you, and that your joy may be full."
–John 15:11

Abiding in Jesus is a life of abundant happiness. As we give more of our hearts to Jesus, we enter into the joy of the Lord. His joy, the full joy of heaven that never runs out, becomes ours. The same way joy on earth connected with the vine and its fruit, so joy is in the Christian that abides in Christ, the heavenly Vine.

We all know what joy is and brings—proof that what we have brings satisfaction. If we do things out of duty, selfishness, or other motives, no one will know what the worth of what we are after or holding is—there's no joy. But when it gives us joy, everyone sees our delight—they know it's a treasure. Nothing is as attractive as joy. A heart that rejoices is far more persuasive than good preaching.

It is an incredible part of a Christian's character: The proof of God's love and blessings is in the joy of God overcoming all our hardships. The joy of the Lord is our strength; we find confidence, courage, and patience in joy. With a joyful heart, there is no work or burden too heavy—God is our strength.

Jesus promises us His own joy: "*My joy.*" The parable we have been following refers to the life His disciples would have when He went up to heaven—joy is His resurrection life. We can see this in John 16:22: "*I will see you again, and your hearts will rejoice, and no one will take your joy from you.*" It was only in the resurrection that this life started, and true joy could be theirs. Only then could these words be fulfilled: "*Therefore God, your God, has anointed you with the oil of gladness beyond your companions*" (Psalm 45:7).

Being crowned was Jesus' heart's delight. It was the joy of a completed work, the joy of a restored relationship with the Father, and the joy of hearts saved. This is what His joy consists of, and we get to share in it by abiding in Him.

Sharing in His victory and redemption gives us faith to say, "Thank God, who causes me to triumph." The fruit of this is joy in the Father's love—nothing to block it if we abide. We also share in the joy of the love for sinners to be born again. Abiding in Christ, these three streams of joy flow into our hearts. If we look back to see what He has done, up to see our reward in the Father's love, or forward as the lost are saved, His joy is ours. With our feet on Calvary, our eyes on the Father's face, and our hands helping sinners home, His joy is ours.

Jesus speaks of an abiding joy that will never stop or be interrupted: "*That my joy may be in you,*" and "*No one will take your joy from you.*" Many Christians can't understand this. Their view is that there are seasons of joy and sorrow. They use Paul as proof that there will be crying, sorrow, and suffering. They haven't seen Paul's evidence of unceasing joy. He understood the paradox of the Christian life as a combination of the bitterness of earth and the joy of heaven happening at the same moment. "*As sorrowful, yet always rejoicing*" (2 Cor 6:10): These words teach us how the joy of Christ can overcome the world's sorrow, for us to be able to sing while we cry, and keep in our hearts a deep joy, even when we face disappointment or difficulties.

There is just one condition: "*I will see you again, and your hearts will rejoice, and no one will take your joy from you.*" Jesus' presence can only bring joy. If we abide in Him, won't our hearts rejoice and be glad? Even if we are crying for the sins and the hearts of others, there is joy in the faith of His power and love to save.

His own joy abides with us, He wants to be full. Jesus spoke three times about a full joy on the night before being crucified. The first is in the parable of the Vine: "*That your joy may be full.*" Understanding the life of the branch in the Vine confirms this. Then He spoke about our prayers being answered: "*Ask, and you will receive, that your joy may be full*" (John 16:24). Answered prayer is not just receiving blessings, but it's a sign of our fellowship with the Father and the Son, to listen to our voice. Understanding that God hears and we receive an answer from the throne is a reason for incredible joy.

The third is: *"These things I speak in the world, that they may have my joy fulfilled in themselves"* (John 17:13). Jesus as High Priest enters the Father's presence for us, to pray and work. This should remove every reason to fear or doubt and give us the confidence of a perfect salvation. If we want the full joy of abiding in Christ found in John 15, and the full joy of prayer in John 16, we must carry on to John 17. There we will hear the words of the prayer that our joy might be full. We will learn the love that prays for us in heaven without ceasing is heard and answered, and His joy that is ours in him.

Christ's own joy: Abiding and complete joy—this is for those who abide in Jesus. Why don't we take hold of this joy? Because we don't believe in it. Abiding in Jesus is seen only as a life of denying ourselves and being sad, instead of the happiest life we can ever have. We forget that self-denial with sadness is because we don't abide, but if we surrender, our faith comes true—the joy of the Lord is ours.

Remember what Jesus says. At the end of the Vine parable, He adds these precious words: *"These things I have spoken to you, that my joy may be in you, and that your joy may be full."* As part of the branch life, the joy is ours—not the first or main part, but as proof that He satisfies every need of our hearts.

Be happy. Cultivate gladness. When your heart feels the joy of the Savior's presence, praise God for it, and seek to hold on to it. When things are not so good, and joy is not vibrant as you would like, still praise God for the life joy he has redeemed you to. His words are still true: "*According to your faith be it done to you*" (Matt 9:29). As you claim all the other gifts in Jesus, claim this one too—not for your own sake, but for His and the Father's glory. "*My joy may be in you;*" "*That they may have my joy fulfilled in themselves*" (John 17:13). These are Jesus' own words. It's impossible to take Him into your heart, and not get His joy too. Therefore, "*Rejoice in the Lord always; again I will say, rejoice*" (Phil 4:4).

STUDY GUIDE

Take time to look back through the chapters, sift through your notes, and see how much has been revealed to you. Don't be discouraged that there is still so much you don't understand, or haven't completely agreed with or come to terms with, the Lord will make this known to you in His time. Instead, be grateful for the insight you have gained, even if it's small.

And if you are in discussion with others, and they seem to know more, be humble enough to listen and learn. Don't measure understanding and knowledge with what God is doing in your heart.

1. What is joy? What is complete or fullness of joy? Are they the same?
2. What is the proof of God's love and blessings in your life?
3. What are the three streams of joy that Murray talks about?

4. Many Christians see only seasons of joy and sorrow, whereas Paul saw them happening simultaneously. What is your view?
5. Murray sees that there is a continuation from John 15 to 16, and then on to 17. What does he mean?
6. How is it possible for Jesus' joy to be mine even when I am busy or going through hardship and pain?
7. Is there joy in your life? Why or why not?

26

AND IN LOVE TO ONE ANOTHER

"This is my commandment, that you love one another as I have loved you."
–John 15:12

"*As the Father has loved me, **so have I** loved you; that you love one another **as I have** loved you*" (John 15:9,12). God became man. His love was in a human heart. It becomes the love between humans. The love that fills heaven can be seen every day here on earth.

"This is my commandment, that you love one another as I have loved you." Jesus often spoke of commandments, but love fulfills the law and includes all the others, which is why it's called His commandment—the new commandment. It's the evidence of the New Covenant, of new life in Jesus Christ. It's the one convincing sign of a disciple:

- "*By this all people will know that you are my disciples*" (John 13:35).
- "*That they also may be in us, so that the world may believe*" (John 17:21).
- "*That they may become perfectly one, so that the world may know that you sent me and loved them even as you loved me*" (John 17:23).

For the Christian who wants perfect fellowship with Jesus, keeping this commandment is proof that he is abiding in Him.

How does this work? We know God is love, and Jesus came to reveal this, not as a belief but as a life. His life, in humility and self-sacrifice, was the example of Godly love. In the way He lived, He showed how God loves. In His love to the unworthy and the ungrateful, humbling Himself as a servant, giving Himself to death, He simply lived and acted out the love that was in God's heart. He lived and died to show us the Father's love.

Just as Jesus showed God's love, we must show His love to the world. We need to prove that Jesus loves people, and in loving fills us with a spiritual love. Living and loving as He did, we are witnesses to the love that gave itself to die. He loved so that even the Jews at Bethany cried, "*See how he loved him!*" (John 11:36). We must live so that people are compelled to say, "See how these Christians love one another."

In our daily contact with each other, we are a display to God, angels, and men. In our love of Jesus to each other, we prove who we belong to. Despite different characters, cultures, languages, or statuses, we must prove that love has made us members of one body. It's taught us to forget and sacrifice self for each other's sake. Our life of love is evidence of Christianity, proof to the world that God sent Jesus, and that He's given us the same love with which He loved Him. This is the most convincing proof.

The love of Christians for each other is central to their love for God and people. Loving and unseen God is the test. It can often become feeling or imagination. Dealing with Christians, love for God is shown in actions as if we were doing them for Him. This is how we see it's true. Love for one another is the flower and fruit of the root. This fruit then becomes the seed of love to all men: Contact and dealings with each other is the school where we are trained and strengthened to love those who are not Christians. It's not just liking them because we have common interests, but with the holy love for those we think are unworthy or unpleasant for Jesus' sake. Love for one another is the obvious link between love for God and people.

The aspects of this brotherly love are seen in Jesus' interactions with the disciples. His forgiveness and tolerance, relying on the measure of seven times seven; His patience and humility as their servant, devoted to their interests; His acceptance of the command, "*You also should do just as I have done to you*" (John 13:15). Following this example, we don't live for ourselves, but for each other.

With kind words, because love does not speak unkindly. To not speak, hear, or think anything evil. That we are more concerned, even jealous, to support other Christians' names and character more than our own. We leave our own honor to the Father and look to honor those He has entrusted to us. In gentleness and loving-kindness, in courtesy and generosity, in self-sacrifice and compassion, the love in our hearts shines as it shone in Jesus' life.

What do you say to being called to love like Jesus? Aren't you excited at the amazing privilege of being an example of Eternal Love? Or are you ready to sigh at how steep the challenge is? Don't sigh that He has called us to be like Jesus in our love, just as He was like the Father in His love. Understand that just as He commanded and taught us about abiding in the Vine, He guarantees us that we only have to abide in Him to be able to love like Him.

Accept the command as a new motivation to abide in Jesus even more. See that abiding in Him is actually abiding in His love—as we're rooted in a love beyond our understanding, we receive it and learn to love. With Jesus abiding in us, the Holy Spirit pours the love of God in our hearts, and we love one another, despite their characters, with a love that is Jesus in us, and not of our own. The command to love one another becomes a joy, not a burden, if it's linked to the command: *"Abide in my love...that you love one another as I have loved you."*

"This is my commandment, that you love one another as I have loved you." Isn't this the fruit Jesus promised we would bear? It's like the grapes of Eshcol, which we can prove to others that the promised land is really good (Numbers 13:23-24). Let's turn all the spiritual language into the way we live and act so that everyone can understand it.

Let our temper be submitted to the love of Jesus: He can make us gentle and patient. Let us lay down our promise to not speak unkindly at His feet. Our daily interactions should be marked by the gentleness that isn't offended, and always thinks better of others. Our aim should be the love that doesn't look out for our own desires but is ready to wash others' feet, or even to give our lives for them. Let self-sacrifice, always studying the welfare of others, and finding our highest joy in blessing others, be how we live.

In doing good, let's surrender ourselves to the guidance of the Holy Spirit. By His grace, the most ordinary life can be changed with heavenly beauty, as godly love shines out through our frail humanity. Praise God! We are called to love as Jesus loves, as God loves.

"Abide in my love...that you love one another as I have loved you." It's possible. The new holy nature we have, growing stronger as we abide in the Vine, can love as He did. Every discovery of the evil of the old nature, every desire to obey the command of our Lord, every experience of the power and joy of loving with Jesus' love, will motivate us to accept the words with new faith: *"Abide in me, and I in you;" "Abide in my love."*

STUDY GUIDE

Self-reflection is not easy. We either skip over certain parts that we'd rather not deal with just yet, or we admit just enough so it looks as though we are vulnerable. Exposing our hearts and character will always be hard for our pride. But remember, it's in our weakness that He is strong; God gives grace to those who will lay down their carefully built walls of self-protection.

Reading Murray's words is one thing, applying them as a magnifying glass to our own lives is where it becomes real. How do we measure up? Where we thought we were okay, we're actually not! But it's there that God is quick to meet us and do His work in rebuilding us into the image of Christ. Don't hold back, come before Him and be open.

1. Why is love the ultimate commandment?
2. What is the proof of keeping this commandment?
3. Jesus lived and acted out the love in God's heart. Are you living and acting out the same?
4. Are there certain people you struggle to love or even like? Why?
5. Murray lists different ways Jesus showed love to His disciples in the interactions he had with them. How do you measure up to these ways in your own dealings with people? Are there some things you find easier to do than others?
6. Look at 1 Corinthians 13. Use it as a checklist or a mirror for your own life.
7. We can try hard to love, but if it's not in us, it will be fake. But when we abide in Jesus, that love begins to flow naturally. Why is this?

THAT YOU MAY NOT SIN

"In him there is no sin. No one who abides in him keeps on sinning."
−1 John 3:5-6.

"Y*ou know,"* Paul said in 1 John 3:5, *"that he appeared in order to take away sins,"* explaining that salvation from sin was the reason Jesus became a man. The taking away not only refers to atonement and freedom from guilt but for deliverance from the power of sin so that Christians no longer do it. Jesus' holiness is the power to make this happen. He allows sinners to enter into a relationship with Him, and their lives become like His. *"In him there is no sin. No one who abides in him keeps on sinning"* (1 John 3:5-6). As long, and as much as we abide, we do not sin. Our holiness has its roots in Jesus' holiness. *"If the root is holy, so are the branches"* (Rom 11:16).

How does this line up with what the Bible teaches about our corrupt human nature or when John says that if we say we have no sin, isn't that sinning? (see 1 John 1:8,10) This verse, if we look at it carefully, will show us.

There is a difference between the two statements. Verse 8 says, "*If we say we have no sin*" and verse 10 says, "*If we say we have not sinned.*" These are not the same, otherwise the second would just be a repetition of the first. Having sin is not the same as doing sin. Having sin is having a sinful nature. Even the holiest Christian must confess each moment that he has sin in him—the flesh, where nothing good lives. Sinning or doing sin is very different: It's giving in to our sinful nature and actually transgressing.

There are two statements for every Christian to make. We still have sin inside of us. Before coming to Jesus, we did many sinful things. We can't say, "I have no sin in me" or "I have never sinned before." If we say we have no sin at present, or that we have not sinned in the past, we deceive ourselves. Even though we have sin in us, there is no confession of doing sin right now. Here, the confession of sinning refers to the past. 1 John 2:2 may refer to present sins, but it is not related. The confession of sin in the past (as Paul did for his role as a persecutor), and the consciousness of still having an evil nature in the present, are part of our humble and joyful praise to Him who keeps us from stumbling.

But how can we, having sin in us—such a powerful sin and strong flesh—not sin? The answer is: "*In him there is no sin. No one who abides in him keeps on sinning.*" When we abide closely and continuously, moment to moment in union with the Lord, He keeps our old nature from having dominion over our hearts.

There are degrees in abiding. With many Christians their abiding is so weak and irregular, that sin keeps coming in and taking control. The promise is: *"For sin will have no dominion over you"* (Rom 6:14). But the command that goes with it is: *"Let not sin therefore reign in your mortal body"* (Rom 6:12). If we claim this promise in faith, we will have the power to obey the command, and sin is kept from taking over. When we're ignorant, have doubts, or are lazy with this promise, the door is open for sin to come in. Then Christians lead a life of continually stumbling and sinning.

But when we enter into a solid relationship and abide in Jesus, the Sinless One, then His life keeps us from transgressing. *"In him there is no sin. No one who abides in him keeps on sinning."* Jesus does save us from our sin—not removing the sinful nature, but by keeping us from giving in to it.

I read about a young lion that could only be controlled or tamed by his keeper. If the keeper was near, you could go to the lion, and he would crouch, with its savage nature still thirsting for blood, but never move. You could put your foot on its neck, as long as the keeper was there. To go in without the keeper would be instant death. It's the same that Christians can have sin, yet not sin. The evil nature, the flesh, is unchanged in its opposition to God, but the abiding presence of Jesus keeps it down. In faith, we commit ourselves to the keeping of the Son of God. We abide in Him and count on Jesus to keep us there. The union and fellowship are the secrets of a holy life: "*In him, there is no sin. No one who abides in him keeps on sinning.*"

If abiding in the Sinless One keeps us from sinning, is it possible to abide continually like this? Can we abide in Jesus, even for one day, that we may be kept from transgressing? In the question, we find the answer.

When Jesus commanded us to abide in Him and promised we would bear fruit and have a mighty prayer life, did He mean something other than a healthy, vigorous, complete union of the branch with the vine? When He promised that as we abide in Him, He would abide in us, did He mean something other than His living in us would bring power and love? Isn't saving us from sin like this bringing glory to Him?

We are kept humble and helpless in the consciousness of our evil nature, watchful and active in the knowledge of its power, dependent and trustful knowing that only His presence can keep the lion down. When Jesus said, "Abide in me, and I in you," He knew we would not be free from the world and its tribulation, or the sinful nature and its temptations, but we would have the grace to completely abide in our Lord. Abiding in Jesus makes it possible to keep from actual sinning, and He makes it possible to abide in Him.

Is this unattainable? Don't be distracted wondering if it's possible to be kept your whole life without sinning. Faith only deals with the present moment. Rather, ask this: As I abide in Him, can Jesus keep me from those sins of my daily life, every moment? The answer is obviously that He can. So, at this present moment, say, "Jesus keeps me now, Jesus saves me now." Surrender yourself to Him believing to be kept abiding, by His own abiding in you. Then go into the next moment, and the following hours, with renewed trust.

As often as you can, in the moments between your busy day, renew your faith in this: Jesus keeps me now, Jesus saves me now. Don't let failure and sin discourage you, but rather urge you more into the safety of abiding in the Sinless One. Abiding is a grace in which you can grow, if you surrender completely, and then persevere expecting much more to come. It's Jesus' work to keep you abiding in Him, and His work to keep you from sinning. It's your work to abide in Him, but as the Vine, He will keep and hold the branch.

He was holy as a human, and He has made a way for you to have that too as you see that there is something even higher and better than being kept from sin. You have the blessing of being a purified vessel, filled with His fullness, that His power, blessing, and glory may be shown through you.

Note

Is Daily Sinning an Inevitable Necessity?

Why is it that when we possess a Saviour whose love and lower are infinite, we are so often filled with fear and despondency? We are wearied and faint in our minds because we do not look steadfastly unto Jesus, the author and finisher of faith, who is set down at the right hand of God—unto Him whose omnipotence embraces both heaven and earth, who is strong and mighty in His feeble saints.

While we remember our weakness, we forget His all-sufficient power. While we acknowledge that apart from Christ we can do nothing, we do not rise to the height or depth of Christian humility: I can do all things through Christ which strengthens me. While we trust in the power of the death of Jesus to cancel the guilt of sin, we do not exercise a reliant and appropriating faith in the omnipotence of the living Saviour to deliver us from the bondage and power of sin in our daily life.

We forget that Christ works in us mightily, and that, one with Him, we possess strength sufficient to overcome every temptation. We are apt either to forget our nothingness, and imagine that in our daily path we can live without sin, that the duties and trials of our everyday life can be performed and borne in our own strength; or we do not avail ourselves of the omnipotence of Jesus, who is able to subdue all things to Himself, and to keep us from the daily infirmities and falls which we are apt to imagine an inevitable necessity.

If we really depended in all things and at all times on Christ, we would in all things and at all times gain the victory through Him whose power is infinite, and who is appointed by the Father to be the Captain of our salvation. Then all our deeds would be wrought, not merely before, but in God. We would then do all things to the glory of the Father, in the all-powerful name of Jesus, who is our sanctification. Remember that unto Him all power is given in heaven and on earth, and live by the constant exercise of faith in His power.

Let us most fully believe that we have and are nothing, that with man it is impossible, that in ourselves we have no life which can bring forth fruit; but that Christ is all—that abiding in Him, and His word dwelling in us, we can bring forth fruit to the glory of the Father–From *Christ and the Church. Sermons by Adolph Saphir.*

STUDY GUIDE

Things may come up in your time of reflection that you are not comfortable sharing with a large group. That's perfectly fine, God's heart is not for us to be shamed. Find one person that you trust and can confide in, especially if it means confessing sins or weaknesses that you have. If they are solid Christians themselves, rooted in God's love, then their compassion to walk with you in your struggles will be real.

If you are not even at that point of sharing yet, make sure that you at least bring it to the Lord openly.

1. What does Jesus' salvation mean to you?
2. What is the difference between having sin and doing sin?
3. Murray talks about degrees of abiding. If you had to measure the degrees of your own abiding in Jesus, where would you be right now?
4. Look at the picture of the young lion and its master. Explain this in terms of the relationship between sin and Jesus in your life.
5. Are you conscious of your sinful nature? Why is this important?
6. Jesus gives us victory over sin. What does this mean?

28

CHRIST AS YOUR STRENGTH

"*All 'power' in heaven and on earth has been given **to me**.*"
–Matthew 28:18 [1]

"*Finally, be strong **in the Lord** and in the strength of his might.*"
–Ephesians. 6:10

"*My power is made perfect in weakness.*"
–2 corinthians 12:9

Many Christians admit they are weak, this is true, but it's a truth often misunderstood and abused. In this, God's thoughts are far above man's thoughts.

We often try to forget our weakness—God wants us to remember and feel it deeply. We want to conquer our weakness and be free of it—God wants us to rest and rejoice in it.

We mourn over our weakness—Jesus teaches us to say, "*I will boast all the more gladly of my weaknesses...I am content with weaknesses*" (2 Cor 12:9-10). We think our weakness is our greatest obstacle to serving God—God tells us that it is the secret of strength and success. Accepting and realizing our weakness opens the way to the strength of Him who said, "*My power is made perfect in weakness.*"

When Jesus was about to go back up to heaven to His rightful place, one of the last things He said was: "*All authority in heaven and on earth has been given to me.*" As man and God, taking His place next to the Father in authority and power was something new, so was being given all power. Omnipotence now belonged to Jesus, and its energy could flow through human nature. He would receive the promise of what His disciples would share: When He ascended, they would also receive heavenly power (Luke 24:49; Acts 1:8). It's in the power of the omnipotent Savior that we must find our strength for life and work.

For ten days, the disciples worshipped and waited before His throne. They expressed their faith in Him as Savior, their adoration of Him as Lord, their love for Him as Friend, their devotion for Him as Master. Jesus was their only thought, love, and delight. Their hearts grew in fellowship with the One on the throne, and when they were prepared, the baptism of power came. It was power within and power around.

They received power for what they were called for—declaring Jesus through their lives and words. For some, it would mean living a holy life, as evidence of heaven and One who came down to earth. The power set up the Kingdom within them, to give them victory over sin and self, to equip them to testify of the power of Jesus on the throne, to make people live as saints in the world. Others would do nothing else but speak in the name of Jesus.

But they all needed and received the gift of power: To prove Jesus had received His Father's Kingdom; all power in heaven and earth had been given to Him, and He gave it to His people as they needed, to live holy lives or be effective in ministry. They received the gift of power to prove that God's Kingdom was not just words, but power. This power within became visible and physical through them. Even those who did not surrender felt it (Acts 2.43; 4:13; 5:13).

What Jesus was to the disciples, He is to us too. Our life and calling are summed up in the words: "*All authority in heaven and on earth has been given to me.*" What He does in and through us, He does with almighty power. What He claims or demands, He works by that same power. Everything He gives is with power. Every blessing, promise, and grace is with power. Everything that comes from Jesus on the throne of power has the stamp of power. The weakest Christian can be confident that when they ask to be kept from sin, to grow in holiness, to bear much fruit, their prayers are answered with divine power. The power is in Jesus; Jesus is ours. We are His members to show that power.

How is this power given? Jesus gives His power to us by giving His life to us. He doesn't see our weak life and provide a little strength to help in our weak efforts. No. Giving His own life to us is how He gives us His power. The Holy Spirit came to the disciples directly from the heart of the risen Lord, bringing down the life of heaven He had entered. So, we are taught to be strong in the Lord and in the power of His might.

When He strengthens us, it's not by taking away our feelings of weakness and swapping them with feeling strong. No, by leaving, and even increasing, our sense of uselessness, He brings with it the knowledge of strength in Him. *"But we have this treasure in jars of clay, to show that the surpassing power belongs to God and not to us"* (2 Cor 4:7). The weakness and strength are side-by-side; as one grows, so does the other, until we understand the verse, *"Therefore I will boast all the more gladly of my weaknesses, so that the power of Christ may rest upon me. For when I am weak, then I am strong"* (2 Cor 12:9-10).

We learn to look at Jesus on the throne, the Omnipotent, as our life. We study Him in His perfection and purity, strength, and glory. It's eternal life living in a glorified person. And when we think of our hearts, and long for holiness, to live pleasing before God, or for power to do His work, we rejoice because Jesus is our life. We are confident that it will work mightily in us for all we need. In big and small things, being kept from sin every moment, or the struggle with temptation, the power of Christ is the measure of our expectation. We live with joy, not because we aren't weak anymore, but because we allow and expect the mighty Savior to work in us.

These practical lessons are simple but precious. The first is that all our strength is in Jesus, just waiting to be used. It's an almighty life ready to flow in according to the measure in which we are open. But even if that flow is strong or weak, it contains all power in heaven and earth through Jesus. We must understand this so that Jesus will be our perfect Savior, whom the Father gave all power. That's why He is qualified to meet our needs: He has all the power of heaven over every power on earth, and in our heart and life.

The second lesson is: This power flows into us as we abide closely with Him. When the relationship is weak, we don't value or look after it, the flow of strength will be weak. When the relationship with Jesus is our main priority, and we sacrifice everything to maintain it, the power will work: "*My power is made perfect in weakness.*" Our only concern must be to abide in Him as our strength. Our only duty is to be strong in the Lord, and in the power of His might.

We must have faith to see the greatness of God's power in us, the same power of the risen and exalted Christ who triumphed over every enemy (Eph. 1: 19-21). Let's agree with God's wonderful setup: All our weakness is ours, all the power in Jesus is available for us as if it were in us. We must have faith to deny ourselves, and place our entire lives at His disposal for Him to work in us. Our faith can confidently rejoice that in everything, His almighty power will perfect His work in us.

As we abide in Jesus, the Holy Spirit will work powerfully in us, and we will also sing, "*The Lord is my strength and my song;*

he has become my salvation" (Psalm 118:14). *"I can do all things through him who strengthens me"* (Phil 4:13).

Note

[1] The word 'authority' is often translated as power. The two ideas are closely linked, and authority as a living divine reality is so inseparable from the power, that I felt I should use the word 'power' here.

STUDY GUIDE

If you are on your own or in a group, give some time to worship. It doesn't have to be a set of prescribed songs led by capable musicians, but rather a time where you lift your voice to God and acknowledge who He is. It can be prayer or song. Worship is one of the moments we can lift Jesus up to His rightful place in our hearts and minds, and see us in our place of need for Him. This is the purpose of hymns and songs, to bring us into a mindful presence of who God really is.

1. Why does God want us to remember our weaknesses? Surely as strong Christians it would be better to forget it and move on into power?
2. What does the word omnipotent mean, and how does this apply to Jesus in our lives?
3. How does Jesus give us power?
4. What are the two lessons that Murray insists we need to learn in terms of strength in Christ?
5. Once again, faith is needed. Why do we need faith for Jesus to be our strength?

6. Do you feel strong or weak as a Christian? Why do you think this is?
7. Read Philippians 4:13 again. This verse is often taken to mean we can do what we want because he has made us strong. But in this context, it does not mean that at all. Read verse 12 and then 13 again.

29

AND NOT IN SELF

"Nothing good dwells in me, that is, in my flesh."
–Romans 7:18.

It's God's privilege to have life in Himself. Seeking life in God is our highest honor. Living for ourselves reveals our foolish, sinful nature. Living for God in Jesus will bring contentment and joy. To deny, hate, forsake, and lose your own life, is the secret of the life of faith. "It is **no longer I** who live, but Christ who lives in me" (Gal 2:20); "**Not I**, but the grace of God that is with me" (1 Cor 15:10): This is the testimony of those who have discovered what it is to give up their own life, and receive the blessed life of Jesus within them. There is no other path to true life, and abiding in Jesus, than the road He took—through death.

When we first become Christians, we often don't see this. In our joy of being forgiven, we feel we should live for Christ, and trust God to help us. But we are still ignorant of how much the flesh opposes God, and refuses to bow to Him. At that stage, we don't know that it's only the surrender to death of our human nature that results in the life of God being revealed in us with power.

Soon after being born again, experiencing failure teaches us that what we know is not enough, and our hearts begin to want to know Him better. He lovingly points us to His cross. With His death as our substitute, we find the key to life for us to also enter into the full experience of Christ. He asks if we are willing to drink the cup that He drank—to be crucified and die with Him. Born again, we are crucified and dead —we already share in His death as a result. But now, we have to agree to what we did not fully understand at the time, to choose to die with Jesus.

This demand is very serious. Many Christians shrink back from it. They hardly understand it. They have grown used to a life of always stumbling, that they hardly desire or expect to be delivered. Holiness, perfect conformity to Jesus, unbroken fellowship with His love, are not part of their Christian lives. With no strong desire to be kept from sinning, and be brought into a close relationship with Jesus, there can be no real thought of being crucified with Him. They are content with Jesus having died on the cross, and won the crown for them they hope to wear.

It's a different story for the Christian that really seeks to abide in Christ. When it comes to surrendering and simple trust, they have learned that their greatest enemy in abiding is **self**. It refuses to give up its will, and in its works, blocks

God's work. Unless self is replaced by the life of Christ, with His willing and working, abiding in Him will be impossible.

He asks, "Are you ready to allow self to die?" Born again, we are already dead to sin and alive to God. But are we ready, in the power of this death, to deny our flesh, let self be crucified, and be kept there until it's completely destroyed? It's a tough question that will cause us to really examine our hearts. Are we prepared to say that our old self no longer has a say in what we do; that it will not be allowed to have a single thought, feeling, wish, or work, however right or natural?

Is this what He actually asks of us? Isn't our human nature God's handiwork, and our natural abilities and skills for His service? Yes, but they need to be sanctified and made holy, and that can only happen when they are not under the power of self, but under the life of Jesus.

This isn't something you can do in your own abilities, even if you desire it and are a Christian. The only way to be made holy is through death. Surrendering yourself as a sacrifice on God's altar as one alive from the dead (Rom.6:13, 7:1), so each talent, gift, and possession must be separated from the power of sin and self, and laid on the altar to be consumed by holy fire. In denying and crucifying self, the gifts and abilities God has given you to serve Him with, can be set free for a complete surrender to God, and offered to Him to be accepted, sanctified, and used.

As long as you are in the flesh, you can't say that self is dead, but when the life of Jesus is allowed to take control, self remains crucified so that it can have ho power over you for a single moment. Jesus becomes your second self.

If you want to abide in Christ, prepare yourself to separate from self, and not allow it to have any control in your heart. If you are willing to step away from self and allow Jesus to become the life in you, your thinking, feeling, and acting, then He is ready to do so. He will be your life, interested, and influential in every moment of your day. He only asks one thing: Come out of self and its life, abide in Jesus and His life, and He will be your life. His holy presence will remove the old life.

Give up self now and forever. If you have never done so because you're afraid you might fail, do it now. He promises His life will take the place of the old life. Even though self is not physically dead, you are indeed dead to self. Self is still strong and living, but it has no power over you. Your renewed nature and new self, born again in Jesus from the dead, are dead to sin and alive to God. Your death in Christ has freed you completely from the control of self: It has no power over you, except when you, in ignorance, laziness, or doubt, agree to its control.

Accept by faith the wonderful position you have in Christ. In Jesus, your life is dead to self, you have been freed from the control of self, and His divine life has taken its place. Confidently step out and plant your foot on the neck of yours and God's enemy. Be of good courage, just believe. Don't be afraid to take the step, and say that you have once and for all given up self to the death for which it has been crucified in Christ (Rom.6:6). Trust Jesus the Crucified One to hold self on the cross, and to fill its place in you with His own resurrection life.

In this faith, abide in Jesus! Hold on to Him. Rest on Him. Hope in Him. Dedicate yourself to Him daily. Freed from the oppressor, you become a conqueror. Recognize the enemy of self, struggling to get free from the cross, tempting you into giving it some freedom, and even deceive you by its natural abilities to serve God. Remember that when self serves God, it's more dangerous than self refusing to obey.

Have a holy fear towards it, and hide yourself in Christ: He is your safety. Abide in Him. He has promised to abide in you. He will teach you to be humble and alert. He will teach you to be happy and trusting. Bring every interest of your life, every power of your nature, all the thoughts, will, and feeling, that makes up life, and trust Him to take the place that self once easily filled. Jesus will take control of you and live in you. In the rest, peace, and grace of the new life, you shall have joy because of the incredible exchange that has been made—leaving self to abide in Jesus.

Note

In his book on sanctification, Marshall emphasizes the danger of Christians trying to be sanctified in the power of the flesh, with the help of Christ, instead of looking for it to Christ alone and receiving it from Him by faith.

He reminds us how there are two natures in the believer, and so two ways of seeking holiness, depending on if we allow the principles of the one or other nature to guide us. The one is the carnal way, where we see all our efforts and resolutions, trusting Christ to help us in doing the work. The other is the spiritual way, where those who have died and can do nothing, have only one care—to receive Christ day by day, and at every step, let Him live and work in them.

Despair of purging the flesh or natural man of its sinful lusts and inclinations, and of practicing holiness by your willing and resolving to do the best that lieth in your own power, and trusting on the grace of God and Christ to help you in such resolutions and endeavors. Rather resolve to trust in Christ to work in you to will and to do by His own power according to His own good pleasure.

They that are convinced of their own sin and misery do commonly first think to tame the flesh, and to subdue and root out its lusts, and to make their corrupt nature to be better-natured and inclined to holiness by their struggling and wrestling with it; and if they can but bring their hearts to a full purpose and resolution to do the best that lieth in them, they hope that by such a resolution they shall be able to achieve great enterprises in the conquests of their lusts and performance of the most difficult duties.

It is the great work of some zealous divines in their preachings and writings to stir up people to this resolution, wherein they place the chiefest turning point from sin to godliness. And they think that this is not contrary to the life of faith, because they trust in the grace of God through Christ to help them in all such resolutions and endeavors. Thus they endeavor to reform their old state and to be made perfect in the flesh, instead of putting it off and walking according to the new state in Christ. They trust on low carnal things for holiness, and upon the acts of their own will, their purposes, resolutions, and endeavors, instead of Christ; and they trust to Christ to help them in this carnal way; whereas true faith would teach them that they are nothing and that they do but labor in vain. –from Chapter 12 of *The Gospel Mystery of Sanctification* by Walter Marshall.

STUDY GUIDE

In any kind of study, unless we apply what we have learned to our own lives, it is head knowledge. Many people, even pastors and theologians, walk around with incredible wisdom and knowledge, but they have very little growth in their hearts. Jesus even warned against this in the Bible, especially with the Pharisees.

This chapter is no different. It's easy to read and acknowledge that Murray says many true things, but unless we admit them in our own lives and see that we need to apply and have room to grow, they will never be true for us.

To really see the power and detrimental effects that self has on our Christian lives, and how Jesus can set us free from it, read *Humility* by Andrew Murray.

1. What do you understand by 'self?'
2. "There is no other path to true life, and abiding in Jesus, than the road He took—through death." What do you understand by this statement?
3. Why do many Christians "shrink back from it?"
4. Murray talks about a death when we are born again,

and another death when we follow Jesus. What is the difference?
5. Even your gifts and talents need to be laid on the altar and sacrificed, why?
6. What are the two different ways of seeking holiness?
7. Look at Luke 9:23. This verse talks about denying ourselves. But it also tells us how often. What is it, and why do you think this is?

CHRIST AS GUARANTEE OF THE COVENANT

"This makes Jesus the guarantor of a better covenant."
–Hebrews 7:22

The Bible says the Old Covenant was faultless, and Israel did not follow it, so God did not recognize them as His own (Heb.8:7-9). It failed to unite Israel and God: Israel had forsaken Him, and He paid no attention to them. So, God promised a New Covenant, effective and perfect in its purpose. To accomplish its goal, it would need to establish God's faithfulness to His people, and His people's faithfulness to God.

The New Covenant was clear that it would achieve both of these objectives. "*I will put my laws into their minds,*"—God makes a way to secure their faithfulness to Him. "*I will remember their sins no more*" (Heb.8:10-12)—He confirms His faithfulness to them. A forgiving God and an obedient people: These are the two parties to be eternally united in the New Covenant.

The most beautiful provision of this New Covenant is who guarantees to fulfill both parts: Jesus. To us, He became the guarantee that God would faithfully fulfill His part, so we could confidently depend upon God to forgive, accept, and never again forsake us. And to God, He became the guarantee that we would faithfully fulfill our part so that God could give us the blessing of the covenant.

The way He fulfills this guarantee is this: He is one with God, with all of God in His human nature, and personally assures us that God will do what He has promised. All that God has is guaranteed to us in Him as a man. And as one with us, having accepted us as members into His own body, He is the guarantee to God that His part of the covenant will be met. All we must be and do is confirmed in Him. It's the glory of the New Covenant that the God-man is its living and eternal security. We can then understand that as much as we abide in Him as the guarantee of the covenant is how much it will be realized in us.

We can understand this more if we look at one of the New Covenant's promises. *"I will make with them an everlasting covenant, that I will not turn away from doing good to them. And I will put the fear of me in their hearts, that they may not turn from me"* (Jer 32:40).

How amazing that the infinite God comes down and meets us in our weakness! He is the Faithful and Unchanging One, whose word is truth. To show us, the beneficiaries of the promise, His consistency, He commits to the covenant that

He will never change: "*I will make with them an everlasting covenant, that I will not turn away from doing good to them.*" How incredible when we realize and take hold of this, and find our rest in the everlasting covenant of the Faithful One!

But in a covenant, there are two parties. And what if we become unfaithful and break the covenant? Provision must be made that this cannot happen and that we also remain faithful. There is no way we can ever promise such a thing. But God comes to provide for this too. He doesn't just promise that He will never turn from His people, but also to put His fear in their hearts, that they won't turn from Him. Not only does He fulfill His own commitments as one of the parties, but He also takes responsibility for the other party too: "*And I will put my Spirit within you, and cause you to walk in my statutes and be careful to obey my rules*" (Ezek. 36:27).

If we can understand this half of the covenant as well, we are blessed! We see that our security is not in a promise we make with God, one that we break again and again. We find a covenant, where God is the guarantee, not just for Himself, but for us too. We understand that our part in this is to accept what God has promised to do, and to expect Him to fulfill the faithfulness of His people to their God: "*I will put the fear of me in their hearts, that they may not turn from me.*"

It's clear to see the role of the guarantor of the covenant, appointed by the Father for its fulfillment. The Father said to Jesus, "*I will give you as a covenant for the people*" (Isa 42:6). And the Holy Spirit confirms that "*all the promises of God find their Yes in him*" (2 Cor 1:20). The Christian that abides in Him has the guarantee that every promise of the covenant will be fulfilled.

Jesus was made a guarantor of a better covenant. Like Melchizedek, Jesus takes on this role (see Heb. 7). Aaron and his sons passed away, but Jesus lives as an eternal priest. He is always praying for us, saving us completely. Because He is the Eternal One, His guarantee of the covenant is effective. Every moment He prays to the Father to secure the powers and blessings of heavenly life for His people. And every moment He assures them that they will receive these gifts. As a guarantor, He never stops praying and presenting us before the Father; He never stops working and revealing the Father within us.

The mystery of the Melchizedek priesthood, which the Hebrews were not able to receive (Heb. 5:10-14), is the mystery of the resurrection life. The glory of Jesus as the guarantor is that He lives forever. He works in the power of an omnipotent life, always praying to the Father to fulfill the covenant in us. He works answering our prayers that we may fulfill our part of the covenant.

Eternal life has no breaks and no interruption. Each moment has the power of eternity in it. Every moment He prays and blesses. He can save completely and perfectly because He is always praying.

It's possible to abide in Jesus every moment because the Eternal Priest is our guarantee. Every moment His prayers go up, the effective answers come down. Because Jesus is the guarantee—"*I will put the fear of me in their hearts, that they may not turn from me*"—He will not leave you alone for one moment. If He does, He is not holding up His part of the covenant. You may doubt, but He cannot be unfaithful. If you just think of Jesus as a High Priest in eternal power, you will have faith to believe that an endless, unchangeable life of abiding in Jesus, is possible and is waiting for you.

When we see and understand what Jesus is to us, the natural result will be to abide in Him. If His life is always before the Father in prayer for us, and answering us from the Father, then abiding every moment is easy and simple. We can simply say, "Jesus, guarantor, keeper, Eternal Savior, in whose life I live, I abide in You." Every moment of need, darkness, or fear, we can say, "High Priest, in the power of an eternal, unchangeable life, I abide in You." And when we are too busy to consciously think of Him, we can trust His guarantee, His never-ending priesthood, effective and powerful to save us and keep us abiding in Him.

STUDY GUIDE

This chapter deals with a topic that many Christians stumble over and get stuck on: The need for two covenants and which one we live under. But the Bible is very clear and simple on this fact. As Murray points out, a New Covenant had to come to replace what the Old one could not accomplish. We are under the New, not the Old.

Understanding this for our own lives is important as we see the reason Jesus came, what He fulfilled, and the way He opened for us to live in Him; all things the Old Covenant could not offer.

The New Covenant by Watchman Nee and *The Believer's New Covenant* by Andrew Murray are just two books that can help you navigate through a topic that needs to be understood better to realize what we have in Christ.

1. Why did the New Covenant have to come?
2. Why is faithfulness such an important part of the covenant?
3. As a guarantor, what is Jesus' role in the covenant?
4. Why is Jesus referred to as a priest in the order of Melchizedek? Why is this different from the Old Covenant priesthood?
5. What does the significance of Jesus being eternal have to do with his role as priest and the covenant?
6. "It's possible to abide in Jesus every moment because the Eternal Priest is our guarantee." What are the ways he does this?
7. What is your view of living in the New Covenant?

31

CHRIST THE GLORIFIED ONE

"Your life is hidden with Christ in God. When Christ who is your life appears, then you also will appear with him in glory."
–Colossians 3:3-4

When we abide in the Crucified One, we learn what it is to be crucified with Him, and dead to sin in Him. When we abide in the Risen and Glorified One, we share in His resurrection life and the glory of heaven. The blessings we receive from our relationship with Jesus in His glorified life are beyond our imaginations.

It's a life of perfect victory and rest. Before His death, Jesus had to suffer and struggle with temptations and sin's attacks. As the Risen One, He triumphed over sin, and as the Glorified One, He entered into the glory of God. When we abide in Him, we see how the power of sin and the flesh are destroyed. Our complete and everlasting deliverance becomes clearer. Rest and peace are the fruit of knowing victory and deliverance have been accomplished. Abiding in Jesus, who has raised us up and set us in heavenly places, we receive that life that comes from the Head and flows into every member of the body.

It's a life of love and holiness. It was important enough for Jesus to mention it a few times to His disciples. Dying on the cross, Jesus was about to return to the Father, and He prayed, *"Father, glorify me in your own presence with the glory that I had with you"* (John 17:5). Abiding in the Glorified One, we realize what the relationship with Jesus on the throne is all about, how the Father's presence is His highest glory, and ours too. We learn how to always be in the Father's presence.

And when Jesus was on earth, He could still be tempted, but in glory, everything is holy, and in perfect harmony with the will of God. So, if we abide in Him, our spirit is sanctified into growing harmony with the Father's will. The heavenly life of Jesus is the power that casts out sin.

It's a life of compassion and activity. Seated on His throne, He gives His gifts and His Spirit, and never stops watching and working for those who are His. We can't abide in the Glorified One without being stirred and strengthened to work: The Spirit and the love of Jesus give us the will and power to be a blessing to others. Jesus went to heaven with the aim to bless abundantly. He does this as the heavenly Vine through His people as His branches. Whoever abides in the Glorified One, bears much fruit, for they receive the Spirit and the power of eternal life of the Lord, and they become a channel for the fulness of Jesus to flow out to bless those around them.

It's a life of expectation and hope. Jesus sits at the right hand of God, expecting His enemies to be made His footstool, looking forward to the time when He shall receive His full reward when His glory will be made known, and His people to be with Him in that glory forever. The hope of Jesus is the hope of His redeemed: "*I will come again and will take you to myself, that where I am you may be also*" (John 14:3). This promise is as precious to Him as it is for us. The joy is the same for the coming bridegroom as it is for the waiting bride. The life of Jesus in glory is one of longing expectation: The full glory only comes when His beloved are with Him.

If we abide closely in Jesus, we will share in this spirit of expectation. Not just for our own happiness, but in allegiance to our King that we long to see in glory, reigning over every enemy, the full revelation of God's everlasting love. "Until He comes," is the watchword of every true Christian. "*When Christ who is your life appears, then you also will appear with him in glory*" (Col 3:4).

We may all understand the promises of His coming a bit differently. To some, it's clear that He's coming very soon to reign on earth, and that is their hope and support. To others, it is the judgment day—the transition from time to eternity, the end of the earth, the beginning of heaven. To finally see their Savior's glory is just as much a joy and strength. It's Jesus coming again and taking us to Himself, Jesus adored as Lord of all—that's the church's center of hope.

It's by abiding in the Glorified One that we will become excited for His coming, which is a true blessing to the heart. Many people are more interested in prophecies and the future than Christ the humble. These often end in arguments, opinions, and condemnation rather than in signs of the coming glory. But it's only humility that's willing to learn from those who have deeper revelations of the truth than us, and love that always speaks tenderly of those who see things differently, and godliness that shows that the Coming One is already our life—these will persuade the church and the world that our faith is not in men's wisdom, but in the power of God.

To testify of the Savior as the Coming One, we must be abiding in and bearing the image of the Glorified One. It's not the accuracy of our opinions, or how passionately we share them, that will prepare us to meet Jesus, only abiding in Him. Then our being changed into glory with Him will be a transfiguration, a breaking and shining out of the glory that had been waiting in us for the day of revelation.

Can a weak human really live in fellowship with the King of glory? Jesus has all power in heaven and earth to maintain that union. The blessing is for those who will trust the Lord for it, who in faith and expectation, continually surrender themselves to be one with Him. It was an act of simple faith when we first surrendered our hearts to the Savior. That faith grows in understanding of God's truth that we are one with Him in His glory. In that same faith, we learn to abandon ourselves completely to Jesus' almighty power and eternal life to keep us.

Because we know that we have the Spirit of God living inside us to show all that Jesus is, we don't see it as a burden or effort, but we allow the divine life to have its way, to do its work. Our faith is the increasing surrender of self, the expectation, and acceptance of everything the Glorified One's love and the power can do. In that faith, continuous fellowship is maintained, and we become more like Him. As with Moses, the fellowship causes us to share in the glory, and life begins to shine with a brightness, not of this world.

This blessed life is ours, for Jesus is ours. We have it inside us in its hidden power, and we have the prospect of its fullest glory before us. May our daily lives be the bright and blessed proof that the hidden power lives in us, preparing us for the glory to be revealed. May our abiding in Christ the Glorified One be our power to live to the glory of the Father, ready to share to the glory of the Son.

AND NOW,

LITTLE CHILDREN,

ABIDE IN HIM,

THAT, WHEN HE SHALL APPEAR, WE MAY HAVE

CONFIDENCE, AND NOT BE ASHAMED

BEFORE HIM AT HIS COMING.

STUDY GUIDE

Congratulations on completing the book, whether you managed to strictly keep to its 31-day intentions or if you did not. The main thing is that you worked through each chapter, digesting some heavy, thought-provoking, and life-changing aspects of Jesus and what He calls us to live.

After this book, don't give up on reading the Bible, studying, and praying every day. This is a lifestyle that Christians are called to live, not out of compulsion, but joy and desire. Take time to spend with Him.

1. What is your understanding of the word 'glory?'
2. Why is Jesus referred to as the "Glorified One?" How is this different from him being called the "Crucified One?"
3. What is our relationship with Jesus on the throne all about?
4. Murray lists a number of aspects of this life. "It's a life of…" Look at each of these and reflect on which ones you have in your life.
5. It's "not the accuracy of our opinions, or how passionately we share them," that will prepare us to meet Jesus when he comes. Why not?
6. Can a weak human, like you and I, live in fellowship with this glorious King? How is that possible?
7. Is there an expectation in your heart for Jesus' return? How does this change your outlook on the day, week, and year before you?

ABOUT ANDREW MURRAY

Andrew Murray is best known for his treasured classics on the Christian life. Having penned over 240 books and tracts, many of these are still circulated and read to this day, one hundred years after his death.

But Murray was more than just a writer, spending his life in the service of God, he achieved some astonishing milestones, founding and directing institutions, leading churches, and traveling to conferences as a teacher and speaker.

Born in 1828, in Graaff Reinet, South Africa, he grew up as one of two sons of a Scottish Dutch Reformed missionary. For his education, Murray attended the University of Aberdeen, graduating with a master's degree, and then studied theology at the University of Utrecht. During his time in Scotland, the revival meetings of Horatius Bonar and William Burns influenced him greatly and would have a lasting effect on his passion for the lost.

After returning to South Africa, he married Emma Rutherford in 1856, starting a family that would grow to consist of eight children. During this time, he pastored churches in different regions of South Africa. Through his preaching and expositions on the Bible, Murray became renowned outside of his local borders and began receiving invitations to meetings and conventions.

The Mission Training Institute at Wellington was created under his tenure, along with Ministers Missionary Union, The Bible and Prayer Union, and the Layman's Mission League. He was also one of the founders of the South African General Mission in 1889, but soon, this outgrew its small confines and merged with other groups to reach the ever-growing need to reach people. His belief in the gifts of the Holy Spirit made him influential in bringing the Pentecostal Movement to South Africa.

But apart from his prolific writing, impactful teaching, and many significant contributions to Christianity in his country and abroad, it's his life that speaks so loudly. When everything else is stripped away, there is evidence that Murray was deeply connected in a relationship with his Lord. As many attested to his life of prayer, devotion, and surrender to the Savior of his soul, Murray would not just understand what it was to abide, but he lived it.

Andrew Murray died in 1917, just before he turned 89, having led a full life in union with Christ, as a branch that bore fruit that still replenishes and feeds many.

"May not a single moment of my life be spent outside the light, love, and joy of God's presence."

REFERENCES

English Standard Version Bible. Wheaton, Ill., Crossway Bibles, 2001.

www.ingramcontent.com/pod-product-compliance
Lightning Source LLC
LaVergne TN
LVHW010205070526
838199LV00062B/4504